Two Braids and a Bang

Diane Murray Ward

Red Penguin Books

ISBN

Print 978-1-63777-721-3

Digital 978-1-63777-720-6

Library of Congress Control Number: 2025907758

For My Family

CONTENTS

Part Two
S'AINT (THE EPISTLE ACCORDING TO S'AINT TANESHA)

Part Three

MUSE NOURISHMENT

Part Four

THE PLAY

Part Five

NONOGRAM

Part Six

DANGA

PREFACE

If you still retain the freedom of reading, please continue. I haven't "defined an audience," you can define yourself since I would not endeavor to label you.

Individual's histories are important, even if libraries don't know how or what to maintain, especially of regular folks which otherwise leaves others to fill in gaps and pretend their research captures large swarths of people they have never met, which until needing a thesis paper probably wouldn't have even bother to consider worth writing about.

This is a book about some of my life I felt worth recapturing because some true archive needs to be written instead of refashioned by anyone else.

Honestly, it's amazing how naïveté shapes one's life. At some point one has to admit, their own incredulousness, and stubbornness. Perhaps there's an inborn unwillingness to accept certain facts about life and people? For example, I learned that the criminal element is not always behind bars and has no need to masquerade in plain sight, because that's why they were hired.

Time, politics, socialization changes both people and edifices. Consider some folks' belief that we are from one tent and therefore one family. I grew up in a house, then an apartment building, then our own house. I didn't know that my apartment building was considered the projects and that a certain connotation was associated with it other than home. My multicultural neighbors and I certainly neither thought nor believed we were other than middle-class. I certainly didn't feel "poor" like children without food, clothes or shelter because my parents provided all of that and more. New clothes were bought every August for school commencement in September. I never starved, was never naked, had new school supplies every year. Easter clothes, Christmas presents, and birthday parties were annual norms. I had elders. These grandparents and aunts, uncles and, cousins knowing them all by name and on sight.

Snippets of my life are amusing, some sad and experiential. Some selections are workshop pieces, all are my original works. Some are siftings for the purpose of understanding living, some ignited from writers prompts or ekphrastic interpretations.

Let me remind you because you already know that there's an uneven wheel grinding upon good people. I've worked with clients and patients some beaten and abused, horrified by sights they witnessed, sacrificed by family, friends, traffickers, some were veterans, and some born differently abled, and so my graduate degree in rehabilitation helped. I believe I made a difference, and I encourage you to use your gifts as well.

My work allows use of God given gifts I humbly use and respectfully now share with you. Peace, DMW

Part One

LIFE LESSONS

Leaving Volcanoes and Landing in Lava

Leaving volcanoes, my blood Carib Indian, African, and Hun beauty-blessed given me not of my own volition, but by them my gene pool meteors, my blood and soul reincarnated by face, body type, maybe occupations, intelligence by reborn, I am, we are them re-birthed. We carry their souls. They are the wind above, beneath and giveth breath, the breath we took out here as within us in the womb. Our womb breath our ancestors bequeath to each of us. Their breath, their beating forms my heart, the multiple hearts of the ancestors. I try to make them proud of this their daughter, their child, theirs, ours and mine spirits combine to make the world family, but first the nucleus of our own nugget-ed sub-atomic sense to build upon the greater, greater goodness . We are part of our ancestors goodness, who always knew we'd embrace the greater cosmos, look to entwine with good and cast off the infected. Always gaining the cleansing the perfection of the positive, the truth, the substrative structure in each of our molecules. Oh our molecules are ancestral and maintain their memories of edens, and lushness, and beauty and waterfalls, birds, lizards, groves, surfs, grace, joy and love; most of all love and community. We exist because we loved each other, came together, procreated and created us. All that energy was not wasted on us. You see we are here my lovelies against familiar tyrannies.

Leaving volcanoes, landing in lava my ancestral religious mixture, is a homogeneous bountiful mosaic and served me through the boat-rides, wavy shores, the slow moving melting of land for years toiled for food, for home. Landing in lava, man-made deceitful and flowing hot and molten some still flowing, some has cooled and said for prosperity mislabeling it as their honest, honorable contribution. Lava some cooled and chipped saved for heritage museums and remembered where we've come and how we stopped, I stopped, together we, me this daughter dammed the flow.

Non-Fiction

Relative Never Met But Known of, Maybe

He was now a widow with small children to raise on the volatile island of his homeland, his birthplace. Known for strength and a combative spirit, this proud warrior was a man strong and proud always considering the future.

Never bending to the invaders, those presuming to be capturers, he fought them and won the honored, blended name of savage. The savages they could not tame as invaders are fond to recollect in their history books.

He provided for his family's freedom, my great-grandfather never caught, never bending the knee, free always. He learned some from them, not all. He learned their languages used his own. He learned of their religion, kept his own.

Now upon widowhood, my great- grandfather decides to take his young family to another island. An island, warm, rich, hilly, with floral seas also laden with fish and waves and coral and white sand to raise his youngsters, and memory of their mother, his wife, his love tears, her memory serving as strength travelling the sea to a new shore.

Hoping not rocky sand, hoping for smooth sailing he works hard fending for his children, the widower with young children. In this process, he relies upon his eldest daughter all of twelve years old the role of new matriarch, the mother-tender of her siblings, my grandma.

Her youngest charge is only two, calls her "Nen-nen" as she neither recalls nor needs any other semblance of mothering. Throughout their trials, joys, children, and arguments, both die as old women. Their endearments through years of trials and joys, and children and arguments and tears and travel to the American mainland, the Carib Indians survival strength remained. This blood within me challenged even today on the isle of Manhattan. Though born on Manhattan to drown me, but my Carib spirit fights oppressions, I remain free, not a captive of my birthplace. I am treated like an immigrant, looked upon as an immigrant and face rocky shores and waves of torment I remain free, not a captive of my birthplace.

I am not that kind of captive. I learned their language and studied others, I learned their religion and studied others. I sail on the train, busses, and ferry to surrounding city owned isles. I am not a savage, yet I still must defend myself from those who try to play the role of present-day captors.

Non-Fiction: Life as prompted by the NYPL Mulberry Library Writers Group

Burnt Sienna on the Left and Maybe Ochre on the Right Today?

Eyebrows were something I thought God gave you as a body part. Eyebrows are also the first line of defense, the dams for your eyes against rain flooding your eyeballs so you can see. It's the way you are supposed to look and keep so that rain does not make your eyelashes stick too much, or so I thought as a kid.

I saw a lady without eyebrows, and I felt sorry for her because I thought maybe she was sick. I mentioned her to my Ma.

Ma said people sometimes removed their eyebrows and use colored pencils to draw them on. You can draw eyebrows on your face? Colored pencils were an integral part of my childhood. I played with colored pencils, crayons, chalk and rainbow markers almost every day. I did not know you could remove eyebrows or would want to. Eyebrows serve a purpose, I thought. This information however explained. the Candy Lady.

Her eyebrows dictated her eyes. Candy Lady's eyebrows were her built-on canvass. Drawing her eyebrows like pointy pyramids without bottoms made her eyes look extra-wide and stretched awake. Other times she drew her eyebrows like waves on the ocean, and sometimes they looked like she forgot or got lazy with one or the other. But there's only two of them, how could you forget one? Fascinating, right?

Drawing her eyebrows as tight, small individual blades of grass or small letter "I's" without the dots on top reminded me of lost piano keys, and the sideways different sized "S'es" looked like parent and baby snakes. Her forehead was a wonder to me. She could use my crayon box if she wanted to; maybe Burnt Sienna on the left and Ochre on the right one day?

I wasn't a big candy eater, but I would go into her particular store just to see what her forehead was doing at least three times a week.

Me and the Candy Lady had a regular back and forth routine

starting with her three opening lines whenever I got up to the counter. I'd get to the counter, and she would say "Little girl." I heard her, but I ignored her. I 'm looking at that forehead.

She'd repeat "Little girl" only the second time she moved in closer and bent down. My inner voice saying "Yes, bring it! What's on today's showcase? I only have a few seconds to study today's brows!" I'd stand there watching her eyebrows to see if they could move on their own now that she gave them life.

She would then always on the third try say "Little girl, do you want to buy some candy?"

In response I'd bang my boney little fried chicken-wing looking forearm on the counter, and with a resounding 'bla-dow" pop open my palm exposing a quarter, yes twenty-five cents.

My inner voice is saying "Yeah, I'm a paying customer, but my ticket price to see that forehead and YOUR eyebrows are the real treat."

She would point to jars of light brown soft caramel squares, white and red striped peppermint balls, slender raspberry and chocolate licorice ropes, cherry sweet and lime-lemony tart discs, irregular-round coconut sugar cakes, orange lollypops, golden peanut brittle, root beer barrels, blackberry gummies, almond nougat logs, paper swirl sticks filled with dissolving grape powder, boxes of chocolate covered raisins, bubble gum, and assorted rainbow candy dots evenly spaced on long rolls of glossy white paper.

My inner voice would say "Lady, pick whatever you want, I don't care! I have to take in your forehead in as much detail as I can in fifteen seconds."

After letting the Candy Lady make three or four selections, I'd pipe up and say "Pretzels rods too please. My change, thank you."

My inner voice is saying "Yeah, because you see I can still do arithmetic and watch your eyebrows at the same time."

I would leave the counter clutching my little paper bag of whatever, still looking back to see if her eyebrows moved to the side of her head and disappear marching or slithering across her temples into her hairline. Wow, THAT would have been cool.
Non-Fiction

Seasonal Help

The front door was always off-limits. All kids knew that. I didn't much care because it was an easy rule for me to keep.

Surprising to me however, this one night, while I was already in bed, my parents came and asked me if I was unlocking the front door.
"Of course." I replied.

"Why? You know not the touch the door." My father said.

I looked at both of them incredulously. I really didn't understand the need for the question. I wanted to say, "Look around!" but I had a feeling that might be considered rude, so I thought this must be a test, and since I already knew the right answer, I answered him.

"Because we don't have a chimney, Daddy." I answered (I'm sure in an obvious sounding tone.)

Both parents just looked at me.
I'm thinking, "What's the matter?"
I thought my parents forgot that this was a special night, so I was helping them by unlocking the door.

I've been good (as always by the way), and while we have this tree it's not complete. Presents are supposed to appear tonight from you know whom. Baby Jesus is used to having presents, and so am I.

"Diane, it's dangerous to have the front door unlocked. Don't touch the door again.
Santa Claus will come in through the window." my father says.

The largest window in our apartment is the living room window. Daddy must be playing with me. (But honestly, I've been curious about this my whole (young) life!)

"He's too fat for the window." I reply.

"Don't touch the door. You hear me (good) right?" (My father was Italian by way of Jamaica, WI. I'm kidding. Some ethnic humor just for you.)

"How does Santa get into our house?" I ask. (I'm thinking…hey, I'm not sleepy anyway. Let's chat. I try to stay awake every year so that I can hear the reindeer and the jingle of the sleigh bells and Santa's "Ho, Ho, Ho." But I never make it.) We could all stay up, have some hot cocoa, and see Santa all together. Why not?

There was one major glitch. This idea was apparently not in my parents' plans.

Also, I realized that this isn't going good for me. Daddy's suddenly upset with me. I hope I'm not blowing a whole year of goodness, for one night of "being bad." But asking a question can't be bad. After all, I was only trying to help them!

Ma says Santa has keys for all the apartments and lets himself in only if the children are asleep, otherwise he won't come into their home.

Oh! So that's why they push "beddy-bye time." Now I get it. But I'm not quite done yet.

"How does he keep the keys straight?" I ask.

"He's Santa, and he know which keys go into which door." Dad replies.

"How does he know who's been good and should get more gifts. "I ask.

"Diane, he has a list. Remember?" my father says.

"Okay. I guess I better go to bed now."

Personally, it would have been better if they said that a giant chimney the length of the entire building suddenly appears in the central hallway and when Santa blinks all the doors open for him and with his elves they go into each apartment, place the gifts, and then shoot up the chimney when they're done. They do this for each apartment building.

That would be cool! But it was just a suggestion. I sent this suggestion to Santa mentally, (as Saint Nicholas) because I figured he controlled this one night only so that when he was running behind schedule, he could slow time down enough to get to every child. That was my explanation for why Christmas Eve was sooooo long.

The next morning, we went to church, had breakfast, and played with our new toys. Sometimes, family came over, and our neighbors too. It was fun. I didn't blow it, but I didn't ask again either. Both me, and baby Jesus were happy.

Non-Fiction

Body Grammar

The "Big Girls" were those already double-digit age. So, when anyone ten years old and up spoke, it was the TRUTH. They knew the world after-all because they were here a while before us. Their words were pronouncements with weight and gravity. They were almost grown wearing knee-hi socks (not anklet socks like us). The "Big Girls" wore training bras and (secretly) lip gloss. They were to us younger kids, street-smart gurus.

My single-digit aged friends and I would co-mingle occasionally with the "Big Girls". One morning in the schoolyard someone within this shared community floated the idea of which of us could be the Virgin Mary. I wasn't going to be outdone. I wanted to be the Virgin Mary. She was Jesus's mother, a good girl, she had faith, she suffered, but ended up in glory and didn't have to die. He's the king of the whole shebang. Oh yeah, I could that, I could be the Virgin Mary. I was contender. But then one of the Big Girls said I couldn't be the Virgin Mary. She said that everybody knows that when little black girls are born, the doctor opens her HYPHEN so it won't hurt and that's why black girls go with boys so young.

I have a hyphen? Where? I heard of the word before in my grammar book along with comma, and question mark. (I didn't know about period yet). I am crushed. I'm a good girl. Now, I can't be the Virgin Mother Mary?

Ma said the tooth fairy keeps baby teeth, maybe Ma kept my hyphen along-side my plastic infant wrist band. If she has my hyphen, I'd like to see it.

As soon as I walked through our door which opened directly onto our living room I yell loudly out "Ma, am I a virgin?" She's in the kitchen. I knew she could hear my question, probably everyone did through these thin apartment walls. "Yes, you are." she responded at a normal register. I shout-out "Are you sure?' I asked again because, I'm not done. "Yes, I'm sure Diane." "Ok".

Now, I walk into the kitchen where Ma is cutting an apple for my afterschool snack. She must be cutting that apple into sixteenths cause she' still cutting a little bright red apple. Very calmly Ma says, "Why do you ask?"

So, I tell her. "The Big Girls said that I can't be the Virgin Mary because everybody knows that doctors take black girls' hyphen when they are born and that's why black girls go with boys' real young." Ma says, "Diane, that's not true. You tell those girls that the same thing they say about little black girls could be turned around and said about any group of people. Someone could turn around and say it about them. It's not true."

I was elated. I was so excited that I could be the Virgin Mary. I couldn't sleep that night. I picked out my school clothes for the next day. I would close and open my eyes and it was still dark out. I couldn't wait to get to that schoolyard.

I run up to the big-girls in the schoolyard and proclaim "My mother said … "What, you told your mother?" one asks, "Yes, I did I replied as I continued uninterrupted," and she said that's not true, I am a virgin and whatever you want to say about black girls anyone could say about any group of people even you, so don't say that again!" Me and my hyphen proudly turned around and marched across the yard to play with other kids.

Non-Fiction

He Didn't Do It Right

Television displayed real things I recognized in my home. Everything from toothpaste, to vacuum cleaners, to toys appeared on television. Toys were especially important because then you knew what to ask Santa for Christmas and on your birthday. I enjoyed television while eating my after-school snack. I thought news reporters were real people. When the weather people spoke, the sky really changed like they predicted. I knew that cartoons were drawn pictures that moved, had music, and the characters spoke with voices so distinct that you knew who was speaking even with your eyes closed!

Our living room window was big, to me. All the windows in the projects were also long and trimmed in light green paint. All the buildings looked the same and had seven floors. A low-chained fence "protected" the lawn that separated my building from the next. But we made a path bisecting the lawn so that we wouldn't have to go the long way around the circle to reach the other side.

I always liked clouds and birds. But looking out the window this afternoon, I was drawn to watch an apartment window in the building across from mine. I noticed a boy dressed in colors that looked somehow familiar to me. He was skipping and running throughout his apartment. I waved frantically hoping he could see me. I even stretched up on my tippy toes in the hopes that he saw me. And although my elbows began to hurt from the strain of trying to keep him in sight, this was going to be worth it! Afterall, his outfit looked pretty good from my vantage point of the fifth floor. He lived on the third floor (or fourth floor?), so this was going to be easy for him!

I figured he'd pick me up, and I'd treat him to candy from the candy store we would have to pass anyway on our way to the playground. It's the least I could do since he was sure to give me a ride.

The window latch was easy to open. It opened inward, and I could easily stand on the window ledge until he came to get me. Since I was skinny and little, I could easily fit pass the window-pane onto the wide window ledge. I would only have to move something over for me to stand on so that I could comfortably get to the latch and prop the window open. I had a plan.

We both had plans.

He opened his window first, and after two steps, easily stood on his window ledge.
Then he did the most amazing thing. He straightened out his cape and smoothed his sleeves.

He flapped his arms, and then he jumped.

Of course, he fell. He fell because he didn't do it right!

I was furious! Superman doesn't straighten his cape. He starts running and just flies. I was stomping! I paced back and forth in our living room.

My Ma was in the next room.

When she entered the living room, she said: "Diane, what are you fussing about?"
My reply: "He didn't do it right!"
Ma replies: "What are you talking about?"
I was too angry to speak! I just pointed towards the window.

Now Ma is dialing 911. I decide to look. The lovely Superman cape was spread on the top of the bushes that surrounded the base of all the buildings. He couldn't be seen. I guessed he was underneath.

I am questioned.
Did I see what happened? Who was the boy? Blah, blah, yak, yak.

Later that day my parents inform me that the bushes broke his fall. He wasn't hurt badly; he just has some scratches. Yeah.

All I kept saying repeatedly was "He didn't do it right!"
Now my parents realize that I think that Superman is real.

The lecture series begins.
First Ma, then Dad, then Ma and Dad, then a break, then there's more double- teaming.
Okay.
We're good.
I remember someone saying, "But Diane you're so bright how could you think Superman is real. People can't really fly. He's make-believe. He's on TV."

Superman is from Krypton. He's not people. End of discussion.

Listen, between you and me, that kid shouldn't have had a cape that stiff. It was a phony costume. Also, he didn't have the real spirit to soar through the air like I would have…right?

Non-Fiction

I Read During Storms

The elevator took its' time coming to the lobby it's true, but I wasn't concerned since I was waiting patiently.

I entered, and therefore thought nothing of the door's slow closing. It would eventually. I wasn't concerned. The elevator had a few floors to climb to my apartment, and since I was always eager to start my homework, (I was already a nerd in elementary school.) I commenced to read.

This elevator was chugging along slowly, stopping on each floor. I didn't particularly mind because I become absorbed when reading. I had a jump on my schoolwork. This is a good thing, right?

The door finally opened on my floor. Her hair was pointing in two directions at once. I've never seen that before!

"Where have you been." she shouted at me? I looked at her, and then the walls and said "Huh?"

She repeated "Where have you been?"

"In the elevator."

"Alone?"

"Yes." She's scaring me. I've never seen Ma like this.

"I've been looking for you!"

"I've been in the elevator reading my book."

Later I found out that Ma ran up and down the stairwells and searched the landings for me. My elevator trip had taken too long!

An adult-accompanied me from the school bus stop from then on.

Non-Fiction

THIS PATCH OF MY WORLD

I never saw a pig roasted on a spit before.
The man rolled out of his 1st floor apartment window.
He looked like he'd done that before. Very nonchalantly he began building something. Oh, he also reached into his window and brought out a whole pig with a stick straight through it.
He was building something.
He had a whole pig, with a stick straight through it.
I continued on my way to school.
When I came home, the pig was roasting on the project's unmanicured, city-owned, chain-linked fenced lawn.
Slowly, lovingly, mahogany brown and glistening was a pig roasting.
Aluminum folding chairs, checkered picnic cloths, red and blue coolers filled with ice, bags with grape, and orange drinks, and beers were at bay in the shade apparently ready replacements as beverages already chilled were drunk.
This festive scene on the projects overgrown grass, filled with dandelions and discarded sandals, also contained a small impromptu dance hall whether one was coupled or single.
The aroma, the laughter, the children blowing bubbles, and the music flowing from the same window from which the man I saw earlier come, changed this patch of my world.
Now he shared with me a glimpse into another world, both his and theirs.
Non- Fiction: Peggy Robles 2019 Workshop Prompt: Narrative form: Places used in unconventional ways and be a witness to the beauty of it.

On White Bread with Mayo or Not

We usually carried our school lunch which always consisted of a sandwich, fruit and drink.
Today we had a sandwich meat I never tasted before.

I returned home before my younger siblings and asked, "What was in our lunch today Ma?"
"Did you like it?" Ma replied.
"Yeah. It was different." I replied.
Ma remains silent for a while then said, "I'm glad you liked it."
"Oh really." I'm thinking.

I look in the refrigerator. Tucked away at the back of a shelf is an unfamiliar wrapped platter.
Yes, kids take inventory of refrigerators. It's part of our job. Let me continue.

Ma is silently watching me.

The platter is double wrapped? Plastic and aluminum?
Isn't that wasteful? Usually, one or the other wraps are sufficient.
The aluminum adds depth and shine while cloaking any color the clear plastic wrap alone would reveal.

Ma's a smart cookie.

Aluminum foil however betrays the irregular sloping curvature apparent on one end. While rounded on one end there is an abrupt and angular edge on the other.
I am now curious and pull this plate out of the refrigerator. It's heavy and clatters on the kitchen table. I begin to unwrap it.
I don't recognize it, and although I've never seen this before, it looks somewhat familiar.

Ma says nothing. I look at this reddish -brown meat from a few angles. "What is this?" Ma replies "Cow's tongue."

"Really?" The taste bud layer is pulled away and once Ma discloses, full actualization occurs. I realize I have an anatomy class on my kitchen table. What joy! This science nerd actualized. Now I'm looking for the musculature that connected the upper end of the tongue to the oral cavity. I am investigating this flesh, no longer thinking of it as a food source, but as a scientist. Mentally I am prepared to underscore my need for a home microscope, and lab in the garage which is constantly disapproved. Maybe I can sneak a piece of this dorsum into school?

My siblings are alighting the stairs. "What's that?" they ask. "Itt's a cowww toonguue." I try to exclaim with my tongue protruding between my teeth.
"What?" they repeat in unison.
I continue paying homage to the cow whose tongue was our lunch. I give her due respect in her language as bilingually as I could. I tried to explain by pointing to mine and (alas) her former lick muscle.
My siblings are smart too by the way.
"Reeeally?" they exclaim. They now talk English with a bovine accent too!

Ma starts referring to us as crazy children.
The next morning, she asked us what we wanted for lunch. We all said in our newly acquired bovine tongue or lingo "peen utt buuuter adn jjelleee."

If Ma ever served us cow tongue again, it was hidden. If cow's tongue provided a souchong, nuanced, layered flavoring accenting meals, it remained silent. Thaank yoouu.
Non-Fiction: Ha, ha.

Mein Librarian

I had just started junior high school which covered grades 7 through 9. I read "The Diary of Anne Frank" in elementary school. Why would someone want to kill Jews? So, I decided that I wanted to read "Mein Kampf" by Adolf Hitler.

I looked up at the librarian seated behind her two- step up raised platform desk. Maybe from this perch she had a greater view of the library than being flush on the ground with the rest of us?

I thought she lived at the library because she was always at that desk whenever I visited. She never smiled. No frivolous ornaments ever appeared on her desk. Neither flowers nor picture frames ever stood there. Her desk held eraser-less stunted pencils and neat, uniformly squared and stacked blank paper sheets approximately 5"x5" each eager to carry a Dewey Decimal number of its' own. As a regular library patron, I knew the power these slips of paper had to propel anyone interested towards aisles of knowledge.

I didn't know the German language, I didn't know if "Mein Kampf" would appear as "My Struggle "but thought that if it kept the German title, she would instruct me how find it in English.

I said, "Where can I find the book "Mein Kampf"?

I repeated and added "Mein Kampf" by Adolf Hitler".

I figured, well she has thousands of books, why would she know right off the cuff what I wanted?

She stared at me. I stared back. Eventually on a white slip of paper she wrote the Dewy Decimal System Number then pointed to the back wall and to the right. Ok.

There was one copy. It was a thick bright orange hardcover book. It wasn't a reference book, and since this was going to be a long read, I could take it out. I brought the book to her desk. I gave her my library card. She stamped the book and as I was walking out, I could still feel her eyes on me. I didn't know why. I lugged this book home and started on the introduction.

Dense. Very, very dense.

I took "Mein Kampf "out of the library four or five times. In-between I would return it and leave it for a few days so that if anyone else wanted to read it, I wouldn't deny them. But it was always there, just one copy. Reading "Mein Kampf" also prevented me from getting other books. Since the book was heavy and challenging to my small frame, I could only take it out and no other books. Hmmm I thought, my struggle.

One afternoon this same librarian who stamped "Mein Kampf" out to me every time asked me "Why are you taking this out?"

"I want to try to understand… what was he thinking? I thought that if I read what he wrote, maybe I could understand." I said.

I never got pass the first twenty pages of "Mein Kampf" when I was in junior high school. I never borrowed it again. I decided that I had challenged myself before I could comprehend it, if ever and apparently never.

Non-Fiction

Instead of following our regular class routine because our teacher gave homework we were expected to submit and review, this substitute teacher always decided to substitute assignments with his own ideas.

For some reason that day, this class period was held in the auditorium; maybe we were going to have an assembly rehearsal or fire drill later? Our class as elementary school seniors sat way in the back, while younger grades were located closer to the auditorium stage.

This substitute teacher was different in the way he talked and walked too. He was always a character. The only man who wore a hat all the time in the school building. I thought only military could do that, and they usually took their hats off too!

He was never as neatly dressed as our regular teachers. He seemed fake. He wore plaid shirts and usually a handkerchief like a short scarf (bandana) around his neck. He was skinny and was always fidgeting.

He also seemed to make a point of having eye contact with me. There was something about him that made me a little nervous, not afraid, but something just "off" about him. My young burgeoning "mother-sense", I didn't know what to call it, was an inner alert, a voice inside me saying "watch him carefully, don't go anywhere alone with him" sensibility had arisen.

Because we were competing with the auditorium echo of other classes, and my class size covered a few rows, he stood up and with a wide-toothed smile said, "For today's class wouldn't it be fun, if we pretended that we are living in the early 1800's?" He's shaking his head affirmatively waving his hands upward trying to get us excited. I raised my hand, stood up and said, "No, why would I want to live back then? Then I'd be a slave. Why would I want to do that?" I briefly glanced at the other black kids in my class. They just stared at me. I didn't bother with the rest of the class. I then looked back at him. I thought to myself "What were eleven-year-old slaves made to do back then?"

We had an eye pupil from student to teacher stare-down. He shot me a bullet-to-the-head look. He looked as if he envisioned strangling me. The class was quiet.

I was dealing with this, the substitute teacher. If he sent me to the Principal's Office I would have said "I'm not playing slave and master."

He stood immobilized. His grin was replaced with a pencil thin line. His eyes were cold, and I did not flinch. He was mad but he didn't dare touch me. He looked as if he wanted to slap me. There were many kids sitting far enough between us that I could get away of I had to. I had a plan if he grabbed me. Bite and kick. Ma and Dad would understand. Bite and kick.

He walked away, maybe told a teacher he wasn't feeling well, and left. He didn't substitute for my class again although I saw him substitute other classes, and because our eyes met again, he just kept on walking.

I got the impression that we knew each other in another life, and he beat me then, and was going to reinforce it now. I wasn't the master ever. He wanted to reinforce his place, and I rebelled back then too. I apparently, still to this day haven't learned his ways and my place in this century. I felt like I ran away back then, and he was still angry about it.

Non-Fiction

Cranes and I Jazz Dance

She moved with a grace reminding me of water, she had a mountainous spirit.

She moved with grace explaining how my hand has a natural curve, my waist follows a stream, and my feet plant as they must.
She had a mountainous spirit.

Then she mentioned her birthplace. She only mentioned it once, that's all I needed because I hadn't known of these places in America. I hadn't met anyone born in a detainee center in California because of their heritage. I already appear as if I could anticipate enslavement, could be enslaved again for I am Black and don't outwardly appear as any other which would only compound my enslavement pool worthy reasonings to some Americans.

Her birth circumstance needs to pain America and not forgotten like the birth pains mothers forgive when bringing their bloodlines into this lifeform. But these are birthing pains to remember, her mother's fears of what could have happened to her baby. "Will she be taken from me?" I thought she may have pondered. The agony of every plantation raped Black woman on so many continents, but oh here, the loss of freedom to birth my dance teacher in peace, surrounded by a different kind of love. The baby in a stable of confinement being born in the camp of her "look-a-likes," "her kind" in this country is similar war strategy against us hued, what?... included my teacher.

I hope I made her proud as I included *ASL with movement, by teaching, choreography, my public performances, and solos. My teacher her daughter named Miwa was just a little girl back then watched us explore dance. I have thought of you my wonderful teacher born in a concentration camp in America. We danced and she taught me through her beautiful non-round eyes.

The air moved out of her way, as she reminded me of water gently carving through mountains of fear, distrust, and racist fears. She saw beautiful strength within my small frame to move others in movement and so I write this as a Tsuru tendu. She remains in my heart to this day. Cranes and I don't need shoes to dance on shores surrounded by pebbles that were once mountains that water lapped through time. Her mother held her in her lap and swathed her softly maintaining her life in an American concentration camp. Her non-round eyes must have momentarily widened, then settled into her natural beauty.

Her grace and mountainous spirit found dancing years later with a then neophyte who now folds cranes with these same hands whose natural curves dance slower while deliberately make not straight-creased but jazzy-fashioned cranes in her honor.

Non-Fiction: An homage to my dance teacher.
** American Sign Language*

Moo

She referred to her as a cow.
It was said derisively I recall, but why?
I guess calling someone a cow is not an endearment. Well. it was said derogatorily as when one is displeased, in a negative context.

She was talking to a child.
So, this child will not grow up thinking of cows lovingly. The child looked as if she was used to the name and went about her business as if this was the norm.

I was dismayed and shocked. I looked sternly at the adult who laughed it off.

I thought to myself, cows don't bother anyone.

Cows chew cud, eat bright, succulent grass and
whatever else cows eat –
I'm a city kid, okay.

Cows have big eyes, udders, and moo.

We use cow's milk
for nourishment, fashion our lattes, swoon over a wide variety for cheeses, butters,
yogurts, and is essential in sauces, custards, and creams.
No cereal with "H-two-Oh"; our childhood oatmeal had milk in it too!

Milk chocolate is good for you even though deep, dark chocolate has more healthy benefits –

Too bad looking dark chocolate hasn't caught on in the white-est of America.
Do you / those only drink white milk, and eat plain cheesecake without distaste and derision too?

Moo.
Cows provide steak tartar. Those would like to filet and eat raw and abuse, and strip and BBQ and rib-eye me, these are pirates of a different sort.

Moo.
A child called a cow, her childhood which should hold treasures, her innocence, her self- worth pirated by name calling from an adult.
Does this child know that cows are revered in some lands, although slaughtered in others?
Well, she knows cows are not revered here.

Non-Fiction

Gradual Awareness

I hadn't noticed him at first. He just kept, appearing. Not too obtrusively, but around. Around me. Around too often, and unexpectedly. Unexpectedly to uncomfortable, uncomfortable to unnerving. Unnerving could become panicky, except that I have a level head. I can take care of myself.

I was aware of the mental and physical benefits of daily walking. An early morning walk set the tone for my challenging and exciting college day. So, instead of taking the bus I walked two miles to the train station. It was a straight route bustling with small business stores on both sides, bisecting a highway intersecting with street traffic, school children and adults of all ages. Everyday purpose-driven people just like me stomping the pavement together was energizing. I purposely allotted this excursion thirty minutes so that I could leisurely enjoy their company. This time-cushion allowed for inevitable train delays. My inviolate "never late to class" record would assuredly remain intact.

He was there again. Was that a shy smile or smirk? No, I decided he smiled, then I forgot about it. It's okay to acknowledge people and go on about your business. I don't recall any exchange, except the shy-like grin, more of a grin than a smile, I think.

So, I walk daily to the train station except during blustery wintry snow. I have three remaining seasons to fully enjoy. Somehow, he's always in my train car. Frequently or always? Standing and smirking. Leering or smiling? Grinning or leering? We just happen to travel at the same time, but I never see him standing on the train platform, otherwise I would go into another car now. He just seems to appear. Standing close by on my train, in my train car, staring at me.

I change my morning habit. I leave earlier. I leave later. He still appears in my train car, looking at me while shifting his weight. Is he leaning and rocking? Is he following me to school? How far? I never see him on campus, but it's huge! How do I avoid him?

If I veer off this walk route, I'll lose the comfort of traffic and people. Regrettably, I have to give them up. I resent him! My routine, my walk is now changed because of his insertion. Now I have to take the bus. I'm about to cry. I don't want the other passengers to see me crying, so I stick my head out of the window. This act serves two purposes though, I don't want my prayers blocked by the bus ceiling. I want uninterrupted straight to heaven discourse with Mother Mary. I want her to see my face facing upward to the clouds and sky now denied me as I ask her what to do!

And there he was.

A few stories up, holding the edge of a window frame, he precariously outstretched three -fourths of his body to preen my walking route.

Jolted, I recoiled. I sat straight, still, and silent. That's how he always knew my schedule. He could watch me for several unobstructed blocks, pass his building, and time my steps.
I'm sure, he didn't look down, he didn't see me.

I went to the police station.

Both officers looked me up and down. They were sizing me up I guess as I explained my purpose for wanting to lodge a complaint or at least something official. No form, no document, no paperwork was forthcoming. Instead, one officer asks me what I was so concerned about. "You're a pretty girl." they chimed. I repeated again what was happening. Then they, depreciating my predicament, shrugging their shoulders, took turns echoing "You're a pretty girl."

Amongst the several permutations I said "He's stalking me. Is there anything you can do? Is there anything I can do?"
One of the officers said, "Has he said anything?" "No, he just leers at me and he's everywhere!" Silence. I said, "So he has to do something more overt before this is taken seriously?"
"Well, I mean, he hasn't broken the law. You're a pretty girl." One officer says.

"So just violating my space, making me feel uncomfortable every day on my way to school means nothing?" One officer grinned. The other officer said, "You're a pretty girl." I left. I walked. Guns were pretty cheap, and licenses pretty easy to obtain. Bullets cost, pretty near nothing. Practice range memberships were pretty reasonable. I was pretty sure I could plea self-defense if I had to.

Imagine walking those two miles towards the train station at night. The stars vying for attention would compete with neon store signs. There'd be a different rush, a slower momentum and harried look on my fellow stompers. A weary, more pleased, less anxious, more tie-relaxed, jacket crumpled walk. I'm pretty sure everybody returns home, sometime. Have you ever noticed how attractive lobbies are? The architecture in some lobbies is pretty amazing.
Non-Fiction

Liszt Needn't Worry About Me

She was a wonderful coworker, and a pianist.

I wanted to learn to play the piano.

Pianos were housed in the university's soundproof basement.

She graciously offered to teach me during our lunch breaks since she had access as a music tutor.

What a beautiful soul!

We entered the soundproof room and there was a Steinway, just like I've seen on television. We had neither a piano in my childhood home, nor one in my adulthood studio apartment. Nonetheless, I was going to learn with future "space bending" in mind.

She proceeded to explain black keys and white keys, notes, and scales. We always started each class with finding Middle C.

Yeah, ok.

A couple of weeks later, we went to the basement and our usual practice room was occupied. She had keys to several rooms, so she selected an alternate one.

Oh, oh different piano. I have a bad feeling. Oh no, and it's not a Steinway, but what, a Krakauer? A piano brand I'm unfamiliar with.

We sit. She asks me to start. Of course, we always start with Middle C. I tell her I can only 1 play on a Steinway. Her eyes squint at me quizzically.

I must confess, my guesses were surprisingly good, until that day. Honestly, I had no clue where Middle C was; all the keys look the same to me, Middle C seemed to be between the "e" and "i" lettering of a Steinway. We agreed the piano was not my instrument.

Alas, the daydream of me and Horowitz sitting side by side, Cliburn meditating on my interpretation, Mehta hanging on every note, Ozawa smiling and flipping his locks, Tilson-Thomas clapping, not going to happen. The tears of relief in their eyes when Security carries me off the stage and the orchestra pits thunderous applause more likely.

Non-Fiction: Sometimes you just must laugh at yourself.

All I Remember is A Lot of Buttons

The crowd was heavy, as expected. The escalator was unloading more and more tourists, thieves and regular folk. First-timers, regulars, and myriad others with just enough fare to get here, gawk and go back without purchasing. Window shoppers are strolling alongside those with "wicked" play-money who can afford exclusive rents, vacations/parties on-demand and three meals every day, yes this mélange constitutes our public. Sightseers on the look-out for the occasional celebrities or dignitaries; all the while clueless of shoplifters abound. Between the latest magazine "have– to- have it" disciples, to the "one day my haute-couture fashion will be here" school students, to the "You call this a sale?" shoppers. They're all here, all excited, a regular potpourri of public consumers and opportunists. Business was brisk and sightings of possible malfeasance were rosy, so this promised to be a non- boring day.

Managerial security staff regularly canvassed the selling floor. They provided added backup to front-line security enforcement staff as myself, while ensuring the establishment that we were strategically located. Situations can escalate and complicate quickly. Dealing with the public isn't easy.

One pickpocket was fingertip-tingling ready to heist a purse ripe for plucking. Placed upon an open oversized tote bag, the purse was prominently displayed on top of other contents. The purse's owner was already self-distracted by the glow of another find. This scenario was a perfect fieldwork assignment, prerequisite exam or extra credit plus for any ageless neophyte perpetrators' *Faganesque* training; a course titled "Rob Me Please 101." One of my supervisors was located to my far right. As I cued him of the pickpocket, he was inconspicuously circling and waiting for "the grab" before moving in. Meanwhile, the escalator is unloading its happy crowd onto the floor. Since my observational chair-stool is intentionally positioned in a very user-friendly location, it's easy to assume that I'm the "information booth and directional guide" for the "post-escalated."

Sometimes problems are avoided or totally abated if you observe situations beginning to brew. This is the public however and sometimes observations aren't enough.

During a glance of the escalator, I saw a father and his two little boys. The boys were mini replicas of the father, one only slightly taller than the other. Very close in age, one could easily presume these kids combined ages totaled less than ten. I thought "How cute."

As they crested the escalator, the smaller child noticed me, and I him. He whispered something to his father, and the father looked at me nodding affirmatively. As they stepped off of the escalator while walking towards me and now within earshot the father said to the smaller child while looking directly at me, "She's even pretty enough for a white man."

I remember stepping forward, and then sudden blankness. I must have shut my eyes for a nano-second because there appeared a pink wall. A pink fabric wall with shiny, reflective, pale-pink buttons co-opted by view. My eyes followed the singular vertically-rowed buttons, pale pink in color like the "ham-hock" that just spoke. I gazed up, and there was my boss pleading with me to please take a break. He stepped between me and "ham-hock". My boss, by invading my personal space, was blocking my view. He didn't want me to step-to the "ham-hock and his little hocks". We stood like this for some time. We must have appeared an interesting sight, my boss and I. "Take as much time as I want?"But it isn't time for my break." I said. "Please, go ahead." he reiterated looking down at me, my head fully upright landing on my shoulders since he was so tall and I was intent upon full-eye contact with someone who could sense my rage.

He overheard "ham-hock" when he moved closer. We knew he would have to fire me since employees are not supposed to respond to customers in-kind. Labeling it "being professional" we were to overlook racial comments from the public and definitely not respond with any physicality. I've had peers fired for defending themselves. The public would flaunt such an advantage several times. So, since he was otherwise always fair with me, and asked my opinion about cases I had, I extended my break on another floor, didn't look for "ham-hock", and lost my perpetrator. Win-win huh?

Non-Fiction

Promise, I Wasn't Looking

Wasn't looking, I promise.
No cage for me, I was a free little hummingbird.
I played where I wanted and flitted about. And on good days I flirted and bounced.

I had flounces and ripples, waves head to toe. And if you were lucky, we'd go for a talk, a mental stroll.
I did well, then "my eggs" started bothering saying "If we become hard-boiled, no babies will be hollering,"
I remained carefree, ready to adopt if I had to, when suddenly I spotted some well-filled jeans and my mind said, "Who's he?"
Still single? What's the matter? I wondered. Well, he could have said the same about me!

Claims I gave him a hard way to go, didn't pay him much attention for I remained busy, always on the go. At first that was true, but romance was in the air, and this was thrilling.
Eventually I showed interest, I didn't want to let on too early that I was internally spinning.

We courted, took our time, he taught me about drinking. When I threatened to study bartender-ing, he started re-thinking. Now over score and ten, he's my love and still thrilling.

And I'm never cold, cause just holding his hand and I'm willing.
We've traveled the city and some warm climes, but never made the corporate climb.

Too honest for most, disliked by a few. Enough to get by now, not elegant but it'll have to do.
We still have each other and our biological child who is kind, cares and minds us for love is what binds. While we rarely

disagree but do sometimes, points of view are healthy, well taken and rarely sway each one's mind.
We don't wonder how we got this far, the grace of God and each other goes far.

This time we meet in America, next in Crete or St Kitts, The Netherlands, Austria, Bengaluru, or Gullah bound ships. Whether meeting in Pembrokeshire, Sa Pa, Lagos de Morena, or Hansou, Port of Dakar, Oslo, Patagonia, or Chile; Kyiv, Venice, Helsinki, Lagos or Manilla, cultures never hinder loves willing.

Through religions, clothing styles, geographical fares, and language differences, we'll still give each other top billing. Wherever we meet again we will sense our past lives, and familiarity will dismiss any worrisome compromise. A soulmate is forever not for just one lifetime, we're blessed to find each other in every setting and clime.
Perhaps, I was passively looking.
Non fiction

Obtaining a PhD Might Present a Problem

I'd like to believe that I would have done well in a highly touted academic institution. My IQ isn't high enough. Dismissing my life experiences, not for being colored of course because we all know that pink is a color.

"My Cambridge" was located on the #13 Bronx Bus route. "My MIT" was located on the subway car littered with paper as my mind in a body with an everlasting tan must be and therefore must be littered with garbage and just must be unreachable; while an empty garbage can was located pristinely nearby, but that was asking too much maybe because the trajectory of placing garbage in a garbage can takes knowledge of physics! Physics like I must have studied from cartoon characters, not high school and undergraduate degree earned books. "My Harvard" was shipped on a forecasted trial size "Forever Stamp" that must have lost its currency on its way.

Remember my IQ isn't high enough and my family would neither "buy" nor "get offered a way to buy" my way anywhere. (On another campus years later, for my dear with an everlasting tan, pinks decided the need for unnecessary remedial study intentionally designed to liquidate all scholarship monies pre-dictated for other colors "to catch up" to pink's ignorance level. A pink gave this away right in front of us. A pink administrator shushed and silenced the naïve pink revealer immediately! But I digress while some wishing my mind would regress.)

Anyway, my "Not You! Ugg" first in-person meeting with an administrator elicited consternation upon my standing when she called my name for my scheduled interview. Her now crinkled brow registered a vexed disbelief and incredibility blatantly unmasked and displayed to all seated in her reception area.

Her ostrich neck stretched attempts to overlook me standing in front of her, thus refusing to acknowledge me now colors the tone of her reception.

Her rigid, stomp-like stance signaling apparent displeasure braces her pursed tight lips which vibrate no longer friendly upon calling my name as the first time when her demeanor, voice, jauntiness, smile was eagerly interview engagement ready.

Her mouth resembles a thin line now. It is through this vice she repeats my name.

Taunted tight, her lips have totally lost their already negligible plumpness and resemble a drawstring purses' point of strangulation.

Is this a forewarning? Looks like my un-signing and the closing of college books.

My apparently "pink" sounding name and "pink" mellifluous phone voice now revealing its host has muted her body's synapses from ambulating and stunts her arm's extension ability; for now, it retracts. And as if suddenly cramped, she refrains from shaking my outstretched hand. In small unfamiliar steps she backwardly re-enters her office, eyeing me in apparent disbelief.

Though not welcomed I follow her and upon taking a seat I comfortably plant myself in her office, anyway. She blooms into hues of tulip pink. The sun shines through her window illuminating her turf as we both take root, glisten, and grow. I asked, "Is there a problem?"

Our phone exchanges were warm, friendly, inviting, and positive. We previously engaged in warm, friendly professional academic phone exchanges. Such was the precursor to this, our first sight of each other was to culminate in my straightforward and simple signing of my scholarship, a formality because I was academically enthusiastically accepted. Yes, I came to the office just to sign off on our communique deemed by our finalizing phone calls thus solidifying my scholarship acceptance.

Now she exudes a perspiring anxiety akin to a precursors threat-felt feeling readying a call for Security. For whom? It's just us two in her office.

She proceeds to question me and my folder as if I am a phony for while I am real, she is having a problem accepting that I am as I appear. This folder, this voice and this name do not match her imagined portrait labeled and framed as me. She is in control obviously flummoxed because my name, my voice, my body, my face, My ME couldn't possibly match my academics, letters of support, etc.

I answer all of her questions delightfully.

Though flustered she finds the words to withdraw financial support due to "sudden monetary shortages."

Now my scholarship is aflame by the sunlight screaming through the window exposing her turf. "My scholarship" I believe is now intended, boxed, and framed for another student on her waiting list. Surely, she has gleaned the knowledge of guarding her enthusiasm and will request a photo from candidates now on. I guess that explains why she wouldn't shake my hand and more. Can't be! Was though.

I am not allowing such uprooting without leaving cuttings and grafting behind!

You see, I did my homework.

She paled when I asked of her stats for tan students. I now lectured and planted my stake "My research shows your markedly underwhelming statistics of tan students in comparison to comparable institutions. Isn't that so? Considerable work needs to be publicly done here. And there is no money you said? Actually, you own X, Y and Z and prospecting AA, BB, and CC with expansion options for VV, and WW presently in discussion." While I continued to school her, she continued to pale. She needed "a tan" in more ways than one!

I left. She called three times within that first week of our face-to-face meeting. I watered my stake by telling her that touted institutions offered me full funding although in reality I never applied to them.

With each subsequent call, she was miraculously finding

money. I'd reconsider but didn't commit. I hung up each time till full monies were guaranteed in writing.

I had faith in this lesson, this journey and in planting seasons. Doses of her prejudice loamed during those years. I limited her attempts to academically deter me by fortifying my nutrient rich resolve.

Adorned in my everlasting tan I've helped many passing through my life's garden; some were fringed, solid, and variegated colored tulips, including pink ones.

Non fiction

"Table Manners"

I tried to pretend that I didn't overhear them as their voices rose, however loud whispering **is intended** to be heard. Sharing a long table, **digesting our workload;** they grouped at one end, me at the other.

Our workloads overlap, congruent goals yet separate. Folders highlighting menu options of hope offerings for persons we aid. Quite different meals with several menu options within our respective folders.

"But look at that head." he nodded to tablemates **holding court seated down at the opposite end of our shared table, followed by their** sideways look, the glancing, we at one long table.

Parts of their voiced menu held exclusion bits, served by their sauce of curiosity spiced with stupidity. Maybe I am being too harsh and need dessert on my plate since it's almost lunchtime.

Mine was a lonely, singular brand, not too hot, not too cold, exactly right temperatured. **Me, the new** employee, a tender morsel, blended **within a casserole of security and self-control.**

"But look at that head." he nodded **again** to tablemates.

I should have expected but resisted clarifying so didn't because I feigned ignorance and naiveté to learn at what point and why was this important to them/us?

Proud of my natural silky waved mane my temple shore flowing over my shoulder blades and cascade draping the rockface of my slender spine as a waterfall, though now piled high.

They couldn't quite figure out what I am what box did I fit in **at least then they would know what column of God's creation laden menu with bountiful blessings I abide.**

But see, I'm not an entrée.

My **ebony crown, twilight colored above my bi-colored eyes twinkling the stars** resembling the blanket of the sky I kiss **and** hope to return to **sprouting** from my scalp like my thoughts **and**

prayers not the bias, the mistrust, the divisionary biases crowning the breeding of balding thoughts.
Conversation of exclusion or inclusion **continued** since loud whispering is **intended** to be **heard.** **So,** I must be an anomaly.
I simmered. Kept working thinking maybe then the conversation and their appetite would be abated with silence.
No, they needed more.
The talk continued, they are from patches of this earth, like me, they are speaking the same language as me, but I looked different. Again, he said "But look at that head!"
Approaching **their end** of our table tilted like a seesaw, weighing my soliloquy carefully. **I offered "The Chef Special of the Day," banquet, side-dish fresh, filleted, served sushi raw which I spoon-fed them by stating:**
"When I walk down the street, you first notice my breasts then my color. Who cares where I come from? **At the end of the day, they couldn't care less, nor wait to hear any accent, because they will hang me from a tree just like everyone else, they couldn't care less whether I'm from here or South Cakka Lackey. Who cares? "**
"Oh, we didn't mean anything."
"Yeah, you did. Don't apologize for being yourself, for saying what you meant, it's ok. Try appreciating that we come in all shades, and textures!"
Not a burb was heard just the wiping of brows and lips. THEY DIGESTED WITHOUT NEED OF ANTACID.
I went back to my end of the table no longer titled and resumed munching my folders. Silent meals offer a plethora of thoughts to bubble up. **I don't think they left the table famished**, their plates now empty, their palates licked clean from such separatist provoking cravings.
Nutrition laden meals are important, don't you think?
Ding! Pick-up, Table 2.

Non fiction

Someone Really Listened By Looking At My Face

I hadn't said a single word.

My demeanor spoke volumes. My gaze, my frown, my brow, my drag, my footstep or lack thereof.
My pain, my distain, my disappointment, my drooped shoulders, my inability to speak and return a good morning. My downcast gaze.

She brightly said "Do not let them take your joy." She is dead now, and her voice ringing in my ears after all these years serves as a constant reminder of this truth.
I have missed her for so many years now. Yet she rings so true by listening she knew, and it was unnecessary for me to respond. My speechless sound loudly echoes through time.

But I was challenged to listen and incorporate as often as possible her wise words; her deeply religious regal pose and practice, her ongoing challenge to me to listen and incorporate and live by and I try to put in practice what her voice told me to listen to her heartfelt and loving message to me. She blessed me by listening to my face, and I never had to say a word.I was only tasked with listening to her. I still do.

For not listening more, I hope I am forgiven, forgiven for being slow for not acknowledging always and every-day the wisdom of her words I need to live by constantly. What is unforgivable is not moving forward always with the lesson.

Non-Fiction

Sideholes

Some people are truly sideholes, no getting around it. You know them.
We tolerate them to a point; sometimes we must be due to our circumstances, their orbit within our forced, prescribed circle.
Sideholes populate large segments of our society. They revel in their boldness, their sanctuary with other sideholes.
There are generations of sideholes.
They gyrate, populate, and sleep eyes wide-open these picket-fence guardians.
They are employed in every settlement, boardroom, executive chamber, town hall meeting, political venue, and roll call.
Sideholes get comfortable and become more callused don't grow any, become impervious and disregard sight, sound, only hearing the roar of self -gratification.
Picket fence points of intersection love their own stink, recruit and with fellow sideholes fill every nook and cranny once holding clean air.
The picket fence guardian's aka sideholes.
They mentor, whitewash, decorate, and colorize. Help each other memorize anthems glorifying clones of themselves no matter who is the next crop of sideholes.
Badges of the flunkey. Dotted holes along their ribcage as they watch the melee, dotted holes along where a spine was supposed to be, all they have is the tail they swing upon.
Well-earned badges of the sideholes.
Parades, applause, hollow-care salute, salute with a boost, "Kiss Whatever Hisses" is the anthem hummed in casual heels, and boots.
Side holes, side holes, side holes not removed. Side holes can populate zoom in worldwide rooms. Sideholes, sideholes are not countered at every move. Exceedingly rare they claim to know no other tune.

Picket fences come down soon, likewise side holes will be removed.
But how would you know? Scared? I'm not. I'm in the organic field, free and hoping for truths.
Side holes, side holes, side holes not removed. Side holes can populate zoom in worldwide rooms. Sideholes, sideholes are not countered at every move. Exceedingly rare they claim to know no other tune.
Why are you scared? Unless you're a side hole looking for a lawyer. Cause you might need one soon.

Metallic Tendrils

The space in front of my face felt thick and caused my left hand to move slowly. How odd. I was trying to raise my right hand.
My vision seemed blurred.
Where are my morning birds?
I was unable to hear even my morning birds.
Morning birds woke me every morning. Their tweeting was a welcome respite from
blaring vehicles and drunk loud mouths.
I welcomed my pre-dawn tweeters, they or perhaps just a talkative one was a beautiful natural alarm clock to my mind and psyche.
The whispering
in my ear was soft almost a buzz, at first almost imperceptible and was an interruption to my tweeter(s) who I expected
each day.
Now I realize that this interrupting interception made me realize how much I took my song/gossip bird(s) for granted.
An underlying sound, I thought it was just my brain humming its own melody, its own static energy, oh it's whispering.
The whispering
became annoying. The whispering became a gradual annoyance because it became louder and more intrusive to my brain. My cranial cavity became clogged, cloudy, muggy, and unclear.
Now I started to breath heavier. I don't usually notice my breathing, like my tweeter(s)again, taken for granted.
My body felt, oh can I capture the feeling as leaden, yes leaden and I was suddenly alarmed. I felt paralyzed which hadn't occurred to me before.
Suddenly a bathing light offered a sign of relief, and a warmth followed by a coolness enveloped me.
My mind suddenly felt calm and was no longer annoyed by this constant underlying whisper.

Suddenly I smelled coffee.

Oh wait, my right arm is leaden again. Abruptly both of my arms are pulled up and forward lifted by suspended shimmering tendrils wrapping my wrists seemingly braced from above. Stronger than they appear these "tendrils" have a cold metal and slippery gel-like feel. Their jellied multicolor gloss almost reflects unidentified movements of forms indistinguishable that breeze nearby. I sense them. And as if on cue, the former whisper clearly resounds "Almost done."

"Swordsfemship"

As a fencer competing in college classes with peers and in community environments
I knew what swashbuckling wasn't.

I was told I was exceptionally good at fencing. Although I felt confident, but I wasn't interested in competing though encouraged others.

I used a foil. Just as others fenced with me and my life. Poking and foiling in both senses of the word. Thrust, parry in the wrist, stance. All ploys used to win. Used to prick, point, hit your target.
Not epee or saber. Just foil. I have a loved one who studied kendo briefly.

I remained with foil. Balance, agility, coordination, attention based. Subtle moves. Strike, a hit, a point, While the tips are plastic coated, I was cut once with the side of a foil and it was sharp, I hadn't realized I was hit. My opponent suddenly stopped when he saw my leg was bleeding. He was so apologetic. A parry deflects an attack! Riposte or my thrust to hit after parry Swordsfemship. Worst when breasts protrude? No, parry deflect, deflect, parry. Petit and appropriately short-armed, my instructor soooo tall was hard for me to hit my lunges against him put me at risk! . He said, your advantage is that you are smaller, can deflect quicker, sidestep quicker use it, and yes, I hit!

So swordsfemship. Used in Iife, from sport to life. A render of the jockeying, I did not employ always,
I forgot the muti-purpose use of that lesson, or did I? Lunge-ing in life. I have been fencing, I have not employed swordsfemship. I just needed know the word for it.

Parry, thrust, it's in the wrist then, but always has been in my fingertips, by writing and reading and writing, and voicing.

Swordsfemship voicing is dangerous. I know, not paying swifter, if it would have been effective. In the wrist attached to these fingers and give voice to record my parry, my thrusts, my hits, my misses, but more often I hope in my future more wins than losses.

Kemlyn Tan Bappe inspired

Clean Slate

Scrub, scrub, some things leave a stain.
Scrub, scrub, some events leave a recurring scab.
Scrub, scrub, the scar doesn't disappear, and you hope will fade.
Scrub for this operation, like a surgeon. a medical scrub.
Clean slate depends upon others thoughts of you as well, some scrubbing means forgiveness, others thinking it's a place to hide, by saying let's have a clean slate; forgiving is not stupidity.
So continue to scrub, scrub, scrub. You are what you are, and you can be different. Ok.
Clean, discard, remove, repeat, show it, live it and become an actualized, clean slate.
For now, scrub, scrub, scrub.

Nothing goes away completely, modifies, and changed, so scrub. We're all scrubbing. Pass the soap, not the lies, pass the truth or stay with the flies, find a time to keep you whole, find the silence that keeps you whole and continue to scrub, gently and with purpose and remain shining and bright. Otherwise stay in your garbage, I don't want any soiling for those who want a clean slate.

Watch and learn from those obtaining a clean slate.
Raw knuckles. Raw emotions. Shredded thoughts now a pasted collage. Picture a slate. Rough and raw no longer bleeding, no longer aching, no longer expecting apologies from scum, no longer or ever expecting accountability.
And bruises heal. Repaired, alive and pulsing freed blood and capillaries rushing nutrient vitamin filled love.

Forgiving is not stupidity but fuel for living, heartily, joyfully, thoughtfully a phoenix melting your evil in her flame.
The pieces of slate in her nest, are scrubbed clean.

Play Dominoes, Chess, Go, Parcheesi or Ludo?

Trusting a world with some doubt, fear yet hope is called trepidation, I think?
Angry at myself for believing in people.
Frustrated with life lessons myself and stumbled chances,
Anxieties with health, no crystal ball to the future, no tea leaves to read.
Isn't it so true, my first kiss with you is all that really mattered?
Being loved and giving, taking and building. Backward steps towards forward thinking, taking pride and being comforting, listening sometimes and hearing selectively, and preaching, assuming and nurturing, Truly, only because our big bang in resounding in the whole universe, was because…
My first kiss with you is all that matters in the cosmos (we felt that sweet, big bang) was all that reality mattered. Chain reaction, physics and crumble, attempt, reapply, savor and gloat over the win, shrug or pretend to shrug off the loss. First move, chess or checkers, dominoes and love.
And through life's journey, all the sights and sighs, and joys and challenge, and love and disappointments, and re-considering and being flexible (literally and figuratively)
There was no holding back, in that first kiss. Subsequent kisses didn't disappoint.
When you are cornered, you really can't "Go" anywhere. You enjoy the capture.
Before you, play the board, change, play power games, genderless all moves are powerful pieces, each on this lie are played strategically. So love is the pawn and kisses erase all points rule.
Same stakes match as likes and dislikes are common connect the dots connectors. Not without that first kiss.
The first kiss was part of that journeys ticket, the long ride, the unknown, the life smack to shared lives and built a beautiful another, with all that what still really matters is that, first, kiss.

You may have to make many, that's life, that's living, that's risking, that's' chance, that's like turning to love. You win you learn no matter the consequence there are books written about your moves, my moves, strategically when to apply, that first kiss. Whatever strategy you know, you strategize through life, loves and woes.

Trust in that first kiss; the ticket to the journey of love, life and shatter trepidation each time. Who's move?

Fixing My Antenna

Electromagnetic waves are invisible in the air, they are static sometimes.
My hair has waves, and I get warning lessons electromagnetically via my internal antenna through waves of people. I don't always listen though' I am stubbornly "nice." Guess what happens when I don't listen to my antenna?
Lessons come whether we want them or not, start as static then waves if you don't learn the lesson.

Lessons are repeated in the people we tend to meet, and gravitate to, because we haven't perfected our guard, we haven't perfected our antenna

My antenna has a short in it.
On my "To Do List," Damn it I need to fix my antenna! I have the calibrating model of antenna. It's near frizzled. So, I have a revamped, model now, a rehabilitated model a better, new, and improved model. I have an upgraded, updated, unstoppable, gonna die one day soon so very alert new anten- ahhh and awake, no longer stupid rehabbed model.
Are adversities the same as struggles? Are unscrupulous people struggles? No, they are lessons. You need to learn or be reminded of the type.

What happens to the one's with followers, the sheep led to slaughter? Eventually they want to be martyred, they want to be victims of circumstance, and others (ahem) treachery, especially the ones that gain followers.
Tweaking my antenna, I knew better. Signals and lines betrayed real reasons, but … there's the rub. Changing the frequency of my antenna. Benefits of the lesson, benefits abound.

Insects have antennae. Antenna attached to electrical equipment can be receivers or transmitters of electromagnetic waves. My hair has waves. I'm not an insect. I'm a human being with anten-ahhh.

When insect minded people cross paths with humans they start tripping on their single-minded mission. They have antennae (pronounced "nay"). I am electromagnetic I have antenna (pronounced "ah").
Insects trying to evolve, tap into human electromagnetic frequencies under the ruse of feigning a need for help, to gain knowledge. But usually they fail because of a lack of maturity. They can't understand the adult concept of worth, gratitude, acceptance, respect.

New model of antenna, new model of thinking, new model of being, antenna, the new kind, the wiser frequency. The fixing, mending, bending, no longer zigzagging interruptus antenna, the motorized, sanitized, lubed antenna, ergonomic, friendly mother bright, taught you twice, never lend support for any price, antenna. Let them expose the price.

Fixing my antenna and changing for the better because the waves in my hair, covering the welters who mask will be sweltering soon enough and get a flash mob belting. Nah, Must be a faulting bend in my antenna because this beautiful brain has thoughts much healthier.
Yep, fixing my anten- ahh.

To Raccoon with Love

Eagerly I arrived appreciative of this summer opportunity to work one-on-one with a nurse and doctor within a Pediatric Emergency Intake Unit.
As I placed my purse within the desk drawer for safeguarding, my first patient appeared.

His shop-tanned muscles rippled propping canals instead of veins. A bundle swamped by the bulk of his forearm was barely visible. Inside was an unmoving, silent infant with a bi-colored face, since the portion brow to chin was much darker than its' tiny forehead. Three tiny round holes were barely visible. The nurse immediately took the bundle behind the curtain to the attending physician located directly behind me.

It's now just me and him.

I'm supposed to greet, get facts for the nurse and doctor, help comfort and try to de-stress parents bringing their child to us for emergency medical attention. The generalized basic introduction is "How can I help you? Your name please, etc., etc." Well, that didn't happen. I didn't remember any of that spiel.

I said, "What happened?' He says something about her crying and then she stopped.

I didn't really hear him since I was distracted by a woman entering the unit. She was wearing a threadbare house dress, appearing perspiration slicked which hung limply on her jutting bones. She looked extremely pale. She could barely stand so she clung to the entrance door. After a few tentative steps she back-slid down an adjoining wall and sat on the floor.
I said again. "What happened?" He says, "She fell." I say, "No

she didn't." His muscles proceeded to delineate themselves into little islands of possible hurt. I didn't stop.

Instead, this high-school intern, four-foot something, ninety pound nothing "Moi" got up into his hot, sweaty face and with finger-pointing for emphasis said "You did this didn't' you? And you back there, pointing to the lady on the floor, "Is this your infant? He beat you too huh?" Her head dropped. Her streaked hair hung like a ringed-out string mop. She remained silent.

I never knew neck muscles consisted of more than 'swallow and speak.' This man had neck veins that would make a beginner phlebotomist's day! He looked down at me and said "What are you going to do about it? I'll give you some too!" He began to breathe in puffs. Puffing fueled his chiseled features transformation into granite. We were both witnessing how I was deepening his "bronze." Now he's glaring and heavily puffing like he's gaining steam. He wants to pulverize me, instead he's erasing his palms life-lines.

The desk separating us is shrinking.

The doctor, infant and nurse return from behind the curtain. I tell the nurse "Call the police. Call Security. He did this!" The nurse is stuttering and looking confused. I'm getting ticked with her.

The doctor informs all of us that the infant's occipital bones are crushed and the veins severally damaged. Her little face with the raccoon dark circles was blood pooling into her eye sockets. She may never see. I really fully look at her this time. Two of the three holes were her nostrils barely visible due to the extensive swelling of her face. The settling blood caused her to appear darker that her forehead. The third hole was her tiny, lipped mouth. The doctor looks at me and takes her back behind the curtain.

I can't move, but I can shout commands. "Where's the police like I asked? Why is security taking so long? I want him arrested. What do I fill out?" I start looking for official letterhead forms, while I hear my heart in my head. The nurse is wringing her hands. She says something about procedures. Sounds to me like she's saying "Blah, blah." At this point, I'm totally done with her. He is ready to topple our desk. "You want some of this?" he says to Moi. I say "Bring it. Some of what you gave her, right? "I say pointing to the woman still sitting on the floor. Now, I realize the desk is a temporary lightweight model. We stare down.

I see the nurse in my peripheral vision. I don't see her picking up the phone receiver, or hitting a secret emergency button, nothing. I want to hurt her now, and she's also bigger than me!
So, I retrieve my purse and say to him "Come on. Meet you outside. You're lucky we're already at the hospital." I think he blinked. I didn't look back. As I passed by, I looked down at the woman still sitting on the floor.

Outside felt good. I'm pacing the concrete sidewalk a few feet from the exit. While my size four penny-loafers build my trench, I'm thinking, he better not punk out. There's a phone directly across the street where I can still scope the exit and call the woman who got me the job. I tell her what happened. She asks me to please leave the area, she's afraid for me, I think. She says I'll get paid for the day and provide me with another post. I grudgingly defer.

Years later I realize this job was the one I held for the shortest duration, and the only one I ever walked out from in my life. In less than ten minutes with my first patient, I threatened a parent, showed no compassion for a battered woman, and walked out on "almost" colleagues.

I have thought about that infant and often wonder if she

survived, for I have revisited that precious infant's face throughout the years. Although this happened before crime scene investigation techniques became television fodder, I have no doubt that I would have left some of him as evidence.

Non fiction

Why Canapé Knives are Not Allowed in Surgeries

Proudly we strutted in our white coats like real resident medical students though only high schoolers. We were teenagers interested in pursuing medical careers who exhibited the educational temerity to partake in this specialized internship program. Within a hospital setting as designated high school interns we had access to various medical disciplines explained to us by hospital staff proud of their specialties. We were encouraged to ask everyone questions and learn from their firsthand experiences what to expect from undergraduate pre-med college course study, medical school and required medical residencies. Perhaps one day, these same specialists might become our future colleagues!

My white coat was always crisp and bright.

On this particular morning, my peers and I were scheduled to accompany a prominent senior medical chief as he conducted his surgical rounds. I was seriously considering neurosurgery as my field. I was so happy and excited that I could barely eat breakfast, so "my intake" only consisted of tea and crackers.

We convened in the hospital's main foyer awash with fast-walking medical and ancillary staffers. We stood at attention semi-circling him. He stated his title, boasted of the extensive surgical team staff that reported to him and their responsibilities. He iterated where he was taking us and what we would experience. My peers and I nodded and smiled acknowledging in uniform affirmation.

He repeated that he was there for "surgical students" which he emphasized as he looked at me. I smiled and nodded again. He sternly asked why I was there. Why did he ask I wondered since I was in the right place.

He raised one hand to the back of his head and shook it, eyes frowning. He proceeded to ask quite indignantly in a disapproving and insultingly dismissive tone, like "She must be kidding! Then he said, "What do YOU think YOU could do as a surgeon?"

This otherwise innocuous question was one I answered several times before, but I never needed vaccinating to respond to it, until now.

He actually smirked. Now he clasped both hands behind his back still waiting for me to answer. He looked to both sides, like where do you think you're going, and does anyone else see what I'm seeing?

The semi-circle shuffled side to side with downcast eyes micro-mapping their patch of foyer floor still compact and solid, not splintering like mine.

Then this senior physician held the back of his head again and dropped his jaw as if I had committed an effrontery, which, I had for being there amongst males; maybe because I was the only female there? Perhaps being female was too much for him. I am also Black enough, but perhaps I was "too enough already" for him to see that I am obviously female. I didn't see anywhere in my neurosurgery notes that Black females needn't apply, so I stood there.

He quizzed me in the front lobby of the hospital, in full view of physicians in white coats and others passing by witnessing this spectacle. He proceeded to ask me again what I was doing there implying we were not proceeding until I answered.

I didn't know how to respond; I was still naive, and I just stared back at him. He questioned no one else. He seemed indignant and insulted that I had the nerve to be there because I was obviously in the wrong "foyer," the wrong entrance, the wrong place, for welcoming entry.

I exposed my innocence, and becoming stripped of my ignorance previously schooled to believe that doctors and scientists didn't view color and my genitalia as "educational editing features" while I was apparently alone in the foyer of the municipal hospital.

My genitalia had a message for his genitalia when he cynically and almost laughingly asked only me what I think I could do as a surgeon so haughtily that I was surprised how caustic he was for he questioned no one else.

At that moment a voice came from beyond me, because the words never came from my brain but from straight out of my mouth that I sensed and heard for the first time when the air around us separated and this voice responded to him reverberating off the semicircle saying straight in his face" So that I could perform vasectomies on people like you!"

Who said that? I thought as I now looked side to side.

Scarlet-faced, he turned and furiously stomped down the center corridor. His reddened bald spot rhythmically bobbing and bedding no doubt familiarly in his collar.

The phalluses remained sheepishly silent in their dinged coats.

Now I am thinking I cannot get residency here ever. He will prevent me and tell his colleagues encircling the world.

Non- fiction.

Paid to be Plaid

How happy you must feel that momentary superiority,
When you think you have arrived, but all you really do is spy
Holier is your pew today, to believe you've vanquished dragons at play
Well, you'll (and I) see what has been roasted; it's your hide that has been broasted
For every time you filet a brother, sister, cousin, and one another,
Your paycheck in the Lord's account amounts to nothing more than sloth
Because you lazily were bribed and are content to smile and chide
You lowlife loved by the Massa, look around at this disaster.
When it's convenient you'll mimic an accent, use some catch words, and admit you eat "that."
But when it comes to showing off, used as advisors, and mimicking your hosts' retorts
I've no wonder that you're nervous; you're out of your element you perverts.

Accepted you will never be, both sides know you'll go for any fee. So, as you pray years later, frail, and vulnerable, no flunkies around acting humble and mumbling, recount your many deceitful pleasures, just remember, by phoniness is how you'll be measured.

Non-Fiction: Some of the vicissitudes of being a civil service employee.

Fault Lines and Moving Plates

Relationships move
    along, some imperceptibly
Others like rock
    slides caused by
thunderous swipes
    secret snides
        well not always
    so secret.
The geology of the mind
is full of fissures so
like matter that
resembles intestines, so like the twists and turns of
languages
The geology of languages
When used for mining
Golden nuggets of silver truths, sometimes silver slivers, sometimes blows up more than intended
Or expected or projected, check their etymology
Be careful with the fault lines of the brain
The moving plates of memories, thoughts
That presumes from one
Lobe to another
The synaptic discourse transverses, which gets your mouth in good trouble sometimes.
The pressure from a lower extremity
that doesn't always pump
fresh oxygenated blood
but depleted and hungry
lacking nurturance.
Fault lines and moving plates,
the Earth's crust and
your crusted speech.

Be careful as you quake!
Brain quakes cause
disastrous relationships,
unmendable, requiring
building materials you
cannot afford because
you exhausted your
former currency.

CP

Sp: Cargos Pendientes
SC: dai chu fei yong
Fr : Accusations en Instance
Ar: al-rassoum maalqa
HC: Chaj Annatant
K: Chengqi boryu jiong
Pol: oplaty w Toku
R: obvinenia vie ozhidan
U: chaqec zir altawa hain
Punj: kharche vichar-adhin han
Hb: wadeantluse vaomedia
It: Accuse Pendenti

Mayoral Mandate
Ar: walaya rais al-baldia
SC: shi zhang shou quan
F: mandat de maitre
K: sljang wiim
HC: mandas moral
P: mandat burmistrza
R:mandat marah
Sp: mandato de la Alcadia
U: mayer ka mandate
Punj: mayoral fatwa
Ital: mandato del sindaco

OVER THIRTY YEARS OF EXPERIENCE
Tur: Otuz yili aşkin deneyim
It: Oltre trent'anni di esperienza
Rom: Peste treizeci de ani de experienţă
Fr : plus de trente ans d'experience
SC : Chaoguo sanshiniande jingyan

Rus :Boleye tridtsati let opyta
Por(Braz): Mais detrinta anos de experiencia

Always fully funded without debate and one expert's immediate approval for immediate compliance.
Greek:Panta chrimatodoteitai pliros choris syzítisi kai énas empeirognómonas engrínei amésos tin ámesi symmórfosi.
It: Sempre completamente finanziato senza dibattito e un esparto di approvazione immediata per la conformità immediata
HC :Toujou finanse totalman san deba ak apwobasyon imedyat yon sèl ekspè pou konfòmite imedya.
Arabic : dayman ma yatimu tamwiluha bialkamil dun munaqashat wamuafaqat fawriat min 'ahad alkhubara' lilaimtithal alfawri
Igbo : Na-enweta ego zuru oke mgbe niile na-enweghi arumuka yana nnabata ozugbo nke otu okachamara maka nnabata ozugbo
Fili : Palaging ganap na pinondohan nang walang debate at isang agarang pag-apruba ng isang eksperto para sa agarang pagsunod

Why? It's COVID!
Fr: Pourquoi? C'est le COVID!
HC: Poukisa? Se COVID!
SC : Wèishéme? Zhè shì xinguān bìngdú!
Gujarati : Sā mātē? Tē kōvida chē!
Korean: Wae? kolonaibnida!
Malayalam: enthukondu? ithu kovid aanu!

This is why we use paid translators.

Over thirty plus years of experience
Ital : onorato ottre trentanni
U: thies saal se ziyadeb aezaz
SC: sans hi duo nian lai de rong yu
Sp: honorado mas de treinta anos

A: takrim akther minn zlathin ama
Fr: honore depuis plus de trente ans
HC: onore pandan trant ane

Or the phony

U: jab tek kah bosus
Ital: fin a fasullo up to bogus
Pol : till falszywy
Fr: jusqu'a ce que bidon until the phony
K: gajjakkaji / / / / /
HC: anken bonn
Ar: hetti wahmiya
H: ad mazuyif
SC: zhǐ dào jiā
Rus: do fictivity do fictitiousness

Good surpasses evil
U: nikki badi par sabqat lay jati he
Pol: dobro przewyzszazto

Truth comes to light eventually
Ar: al-haqiqal tadhar fe nahaya mattaf
Rus: Istina rano ili pozdno stanovitsya izvestnoy
Fr: La vérité finit par éclater au grand jour
JP : Shinjitsu wa yagate akasareru

God sees all
Ital: Dio vede tutto

Good to pray
Tad.Ch.: hao hao qi dao
SC: Hao qidao
Fr: bon de prier
Pun: Prarathana karana lai caga

Ig : odi mma ikpe ekpere

You played your part.
Y: du hast geshfilt deyn khlk
Sp: Usted jugó su papel
Fr: Vous avez joué votre rôle

A higher source is in play
Dutch: er ii seen hogere bron in het-spel
HC: yon sous ki pi wo se nanjwe
It: È in gioco una sorgente piu alta

Understood?
Ar: fahimtu?
Pol: Zrozumiano?
Rus:Ponyatno ?
HC: Konprann?
Sp: ¿ Entendido ?
SC: Míngbái le ma ?

Not yet? Wait.
K: ajig anim? Gi dalida
Rus: Yeshche net? Podozhdi
Ital: Non ancora ? Aspettate.
Fr: Pas encore ? Attendez.

Do we have to do all of these languages? Really?
Pol: Czy musimy znać wszystkie te języki ?
Ch: Wŏmen bixū xuéhuì suŏyŏu zhèhiē yúyán ma ?

Required?
Gr: Apaiteítai?
It: Enecessario?
HC: Obigatwa?
Ger: Erforderlich ?

Sp: ¿ Es necesario ?

Mandatory COVID information in all of these languages! Immediately? Without debate / delay / budgetary estimation can wait till…
Now do you see why we trust and value professional translation services?
Maybe not. Why would you?
Non fiction

What Keeps Me Going?

A child's smile, and infectious laughter
My husband's dimples and swagger
Our son's eyes, curls and knowing grin.
My siblings' voices, individuality, and humor.
Parental and elder concerns expressed; their childhood memories and recipes shared.
Sane friends.
Continuous seasonless "Spring cleaning" of family and acquaintances.
Meeting new poets.
Writing with depth and purpose, breathing, loving, T'ai Chi, music, artisan work,
Limited hope, no longer abundant, tempered by reality, ageing, gaining sense,
Trying to obtain wisdom, just on the cusp of obtaining wisdom, or I'm fooling myself. Well, it'll play out or not. Wisdom is elusive or I've attained some by this writing and documenting thoughts, ideas, constructive positive habits I have included in my life.
What Keeps Me Going?
Listening and not saying much anymore, keeping a more concerted silence so that I can relish the gifts that may unfold in my stillness. Identifying disingenuous persons and leaving them alone to learn on their own and not at my expense because they value me less than they value themselves.
"What keeps me going" is the adventure of your mind and mine engaging in the unknown oftentimes in synch and tantalizingly when not in-synch at all. Maybe I'm hearing wisdom bells, its sounds like music humming, low, rhythmic, hypnotic, welcoming, comforting. Note it. Continue, try to sing along. Not ready, yet? Still tuning my sinews, my neurons, my heart.

Benicia California First Tuesday Writers Group prompt and my response.

Chicken P.O.C.'s

Ethics is a luxury for Europeans, and a necessity for P.O.C.?
Ethics is a frivolity for Europeans and essential for P.O.C.?

Ethics is an exercise, an experiment, a concept to be observed
and dabbled with once in a whole while.

A mantra whenever you're feeling carefree and moody.

Trying to be with it, with the people, trying to prove non-biased.
Oh yeah, trying to prove yourself until you get real and a job
that pays and not pull your own that are a threat.

Wholeness obscured, pretending one with every people; just
waiting to pull a signature in your temporary memory and
permanent moment.

Without ethics you get caught? Really? You non – European?
With ethics you'd get pulled down, Huh? Nonetheless you have
your honors and remain non-ostracized.

I Breathed Them In

For all the lies C gave us to return …
And the soot of bodies and machinery we inhaled …
For all the lies C swore to and she is living prettier far away from the aftermath

For all the masks distributed that we shouldn't have worn all day long, full tours that were only good for three or four hours
For all the lies C representing the government gave us to return, and it continues for all the quirky ventilation, the lies Government continues to tell, explained conveniently from far away.
For all the lies C gave us, and her cohorts, still today they expound and make hundreds of "matter."
Thousands of dollars yearly to add to their coffers and care less about our lives which don't matter.

To those on registries of various pretend government caring, we are just statistics and expendable, expendable, and they go on unchecked, fake, healthy, blazoned as what heroes, got everyone back, the dust, the soot, the clearing the soaking the streets, no watering them down to keep the dust that rose every day, sent to Isle for removing, all temporary, upon return the air still was different, mixed with body dust, air conditioner dust, particles of people floating in your nostrils the epicenter spread and as cleaning windows dropped down the angels flesh, each pore, each pore, each last breath lingered above us in the trenches, keeping the everyday to appease the government that lied, and lies and pretends and could care less about what you breathe, because they lied and as you have the nerve to be a survivor, you survive the horror, the unbelief, the vivid running, escape, no service, do not panic, try to communicate, seek out ways to escape, but wind has fleeter foot and sky no longer clear, blue, it was that clear morning, and the blue became grayer each subsequent day, weak, month, year.

Decade. Score. More come. Puff, cough, sneeze, wheeze. Inhaled and not exchanged for new. Stayed, remained. Never left me, so no need to return the gift of lies.
Non-Fiction: I am a 911 Survivor

Good To Go, Got My Armor On

I'm going out and need to make sure I have my emergency
funds available when I'm ready to leave this rally for the next
one later tonight. I'm listening to their conversation, but I'm
beyond this argument. Our next steps, where are we going from
here? Who has new ideas? Strategies?
I need fresh air, fresh perspectives!
Next rally. New spots, new neighborhoods, different outlook –
all comes down to strategies my people.
We will always look good when we fight in case the newspapers
and photographers arrive.
My voice will be supported by these clear spoken lips, slick,
neatly and attractively dressed sister, yes right here me, ready to
be interviewed on the spot with my take, ideas, visions, hopes,
fears, misgivings and mostly my solutions because I'm ready.
I'm presentable for TV, I'm poised for radio, I'm non-threatening,
huh, appearing. Bring it. You don't know me yet!
*Ekphrastic response to Dr. Doris Derby 's photograph Erwin Family
Farm, Mississippi 1969*

YOU ARE MY KEEPSAKE

I carry my keepsake
        within my mind
        and my comments
In order to activate my
        keepsake
        I, no, it triggers itself
        awake like when I'm about
        to make a misstep or
        say a regrettable
phrase.
        I carry my keepsake or does
        my keepsake carry me?
        My keepsake is my moral
        barometer because my
keepsake is my moral
barometer. My ancestral
"you know better, don't be
baited" barometer so
engraved in their blood,
sweat, blood, tears, weary
bleary eyed and laughter
we fulfilled degrees
eyes.
I carry my keepsake
in my behavior
as a suit that forms
my body of thought,
beliefs, attitude and
reflection.

This culmination I am
not always a-tuned to

redirects my synapse
into a channel
directly into my
vocal chords and my
stance, my body
language, my tilt
my pitch, tone, voice
and there alive.
You are all alive again
as snippets of you
never die, and I
become maybe a
keepsake to the
next generation.

Non-Fiction: A Between The Lines prompt. One can only hope some generational positives will endure.

Tally Your Gains

You didn't find what wasn't lost, unless you were the one that was lost.
Now you've found yourself to talk to huh.
Are you finding what you lost? Now you've found the real you.
Like what you see, believe, hold dear?
Have you lost your biases, or found a few?
Have you found redemption or loss your faith?
Have you lost the conscience you never had, or finally found one?
Did you lose weight and find yourself satiated from a spiritual manna?
Did you really lose anything, but gained so, so much more?
You zoom around the globe now in hyper speed. Emergency resuscitation is still in the works because hands can virtually clasp across the screen.
True poet friends and creatives don't require explanations/justifications to the nosey and insecure because your wordsmithing is more than sufficient.
Have you lost any fights and gained well deserved bruising? Is that your judgmental self-calling?
Have you found your voice at the expense of others? Oh, so no change. You weathered this well. Another unseen monster wins another bout.
People don't want to necessarily be other than they are so why change when you can get attention? Play the victim while becoming the victimizer, the bully for a change. And when you have no takers continue grinning because your fall is coming. It's the fulcrum of life. The alleged Ying/Yang, the equalizing, the KARMA unless you're all above that as well. Aren't you super powerful?
Is there a palpable elixir? I wondered.

I lost a fair portion of my sense of humor. I found an ability to silently cry deeper about the extinctions of animals, plants and my belief that people are intrinsically good when they aren't.

I found out how sinister people can be and smile at the same time, but I found that out pre-pandemic. I needed reminding to the nth degree during the pandemic.

I lost a fair portion of my belief that people are mostly kind, fair, good natured, believe in God and will suffer from evil intentions. No.

I found my innate inborn instincts again that I denied via the intentional confusion of mean-spirited persons. They faked being familiar but found them to be pore-covered water-retentive shells with faulty-internal plumbing.

I beautifully lost those negators so that room could be made for gain. For those lost were meant to be lost at a specific time as newfound lessons, fortifying strength and replacing space. Yes, leaving spaces that were empty and filling with new steps to take,

Continually filling, continually removing, replacing broken shells with new plumbing, finding what is worthwhile and letting go of what isn't repurposed, rehabbed and recyclable. I track what's left, continue in "the found" and relish it for beneficial use.

Fiction: New York Public Library ZINE 2022 Theme "LOST /FOUND" SUBMISSION

HABIT

Tweenagers, those between the ages of 13- 19, are open to learning new material. Those years were exciting, sometimes difficult, troublesome, and hormonal for us as well when we were those ages.

I was the new 7th and 8th Grade history/social studies teacher. My students were from this predominately Hispanic, Caribbean and Black neighborhood.

I was a 5-foot-tall size five. To add illusionary height, I upswept my hair and wore 1.5-inch heels. Still, some of my students where already taller and more buxom than me, others were not, but getting there. My natural enhancement period had already expired.

I was the type of teacher that expected student's homework at least attempted if not completed, assigned chapters read, perhaps even read ahead of my assigning, I expected students to study for tests, be attentive and respectful, not disruptive. I hoped that students who consider going to Detention a badge of honor were not influential. I retained students' secrets just between us unless I thought harm would befall them and I would intercede only with their permission.

The tweenager years provide testing experience for some would-be bullies. A couple of times after school, one or two students would accompany me to the bus stop, claiming their escort was to assure them that I was going home. They would say, once or twice, "You're lucky you don't have a car, we would have flattened your tires! Go on home!" I secretly prayed that these tweenagers would turn their negative aggression into brilliant thought and productive genius one day.

Students attending this primary grade school were required to wear uniforms. Each morning began with the recitation of the Pledge of Allegiance to the American flag and since this was a Catholic school an inspirational prayer as well. A different student was selected each day for this honor which they delivered proudly from the Principals' Office. The Principals' Office housed the public address system allowing for our unison pledging, praying and immediate emergency broadcasting since all classrooms contained an overhead speaker.

The Principal and Assistant Principal were both nuns, while all teachers were lay instructors. You didn't have to be Catholic to teach there, but it was understood as an instructor that you would teach Catholic Christian lessons during scheduled school periods on designated days each week.

Students were Christian, or at least their parents/guardians agreed to the requirement of having a religion class as part of the curriculum. As instructors, we prepared and submitted all lesson plans for every subject equally requiring administrative review and signed approval prior to their presentation.

Teachers were available for students requesting remedial assistance. The curriculum was constantly checked and reviewed for substantive material within educational guidelines and expectations legally and parentally.

Eighth graders constituted the graduating class. This was Springtime and all eighth graders were expected to attend new schools in the Fall.

The time came for me to teach the lesson plan I wrote concerning Adam and Eve. Formed by God they are parents of all humankind, and due to their disobedience cast out of the Garden of Eden. I'm paraphrasing.

Honestly, on this particular day, I wasn't feeling it. You know, teachers, our enthusiasm is infectious to our students; that's why we give our best. It's our nature, we habitually try to engage our students in every topic we teach.

So, I addressed the class and said "Everyone here, I mean you're all familiar with the Adam and Eve story, right? You've heard this every year, right?" They all shook their heads affirmatively. The entire class, approximately 30 +students shook their heads affirmatively.

Well, their response ignited my faith! I went ROGUE!

Testing the waters, I asked the class if anyone has ever heard of Beijing aka Peking Man. Nada?

I wrote the word Anthropology on the blackboard. I wrote Darwin's name on the blackboard, then Synanthropic Pekinese, Australopithecus, and Neanderthal Man.

My high heels helped me reach the higher parts of the blackboard I didn't usually use, but I needed more space, as my arm flew across the blackboard charting centuries, millennium of … evolutionary theory and conjecture. Words were racing across the blackboard expanse including the names of archeological prophets like the Leakey's!

My students appeared stunned. No noise, no talking, just the gliding soft sound of pens and pencils trying to copy every word, I even heard a student resharpening their pencil! My students were taking notes, furiously and curiously writing to keep up with me. Every time I turned around, they were staring at me, all eyes-wide attentive, and not slouching!

Some just listening to my voice appearing to imagine these revelations, not like the chapter in the Bible.

I saw bird's beak-shut sitting on the window ledge! **I held class!**

As my arm shifted across the Serengeti Plain and landing on the bi-pedal ancestral treasures of Olduvai Gorge I suddenly heard a voice hovering from above my shoulder where my Guardian Angel usually reposes, and this voice says:

"Miss Murray, Would you come to my office please?"

Eeeeeee! In unison the chalk in my hand made the same screeching sound as my pre-frontal lobe. Oh darn, I forgot that each classrooms' speaker system could be tuned to individual classrooms and listened to by the Principal unannounced.

A few students took this opportunity to exhibit "devolving tendencies" and leaping out of their seats howled OOOOOH, I never heard a teacher called to the Principal's Office before! You're in trouble! "Owww, you are getting fired! I'll help you pack. She's gone. Bye-bye. See yah. Wahhh! Miss you already! Door over there! She's gone! Whoop! "

As consummate teachers what do we do when we are called away suddenly for an emergency? You would do as I did. We place "busy work" on the blackboard knowing full well they won't do it, well maybe two or three will, then you ask a fellow teacher from across the hall to spot check your class every few minutes.

As I descend the stairs to the" Principal Gallows," I am mentally constructing a checklist of personal belongings: a sweater, emergency umbrella, and a book I always retain for leisure reading. Now I have to seek employment and explain a time gap since a reference letter may not be forthcoming.

Upon entering her office, I find the Principal standing beside her desk with the Assistant Principal seated nearby. The Assistant Principal is the younger of the two nuns. She's not crazy about me and seems to frown all the time. They are of the same religious order. They share love of Christ, this school and students. They do not share the same like of me for some reason. The older one and I always seem to connect, she's cool, and thank God she's the head honcho, the Principal. but what can I do? I was not teaching the Adam and Eve lesson plan she approved. Yes, that was me. Rogue teacher! Called to the Principal's Office, by the Nun Principal on the classroom speaker!

Nun Principal did not offer me a seat, we both stood while the Nun Assistant Principal remained seated.

Nun Principal said "I heard your class just now on Evolution. Do you think they understood it?

Me: "I don't know, they seem to be listening, and they were taking notes. "

Nun Principal replied: "Repeat it tomorrow."

Me: "Excuse me Sister."

Nun Principal: "Repeat the same class tomorrow. Make sure they understand this material. They are going into the world now. They need to hear this from us and be prepared because there is so much for them to learn, and we must not keep anything from them. We must expose them to the world, and we can't have them go into the world of learning without knowing that we informed them of this when we felt they could understand."

Nun Assistant Principal doesn't appear too pleased. In fact, she remains silent as I leave the office.

I jauntily alight the stairs, return to my classroom and announce "Quiz on this material Friday. Suggest you take notes, since I'm adding this grade on your next report card."

"Whaaaat! She's not going?"

I continue" Whoever completed the work I left on the board gets extra credit. Who completed it? "

Ah yes, many hands are raised.

I heard a few moans; saw many smiles and we are rolling! My

class and I are going to invent the wheel, meantime, I'm walking talk, clicking my heels.

I repeated and enhanced this lesson many times for I am not alone in helping young minds gain knowledge, consider alternate ways of thinking, and evolving.

Nun Principal and I share a vision of expansive education. Some of us find gaps between faith, science, and knowledge. We ambulate to find a comfortable, safe, non-judgmental coexistence for strong beliefs that can either nurture each other or respectfully accept their difference. We work towards peaceful coexistence, not alienation or altercation.

My Nun Principal was steering this school like an ark holding precious species towards land and light, because for some of us, it's our habit.

Non-Fiction, St Augustine's, South Bronx

Laughter

Start with what makes me smile. Dig into that thought, theory to find my "funny bone".
Continue with smart sarcasm, pithy verbiage
Add a dose of mirth or double- entendé.
Consider mood change or abrupt twist to the punchline.
Bind in a deadpan soundtrack that will either disgust or thrill me and heighten the suspense of waiting for the "other shoe to drop".
Do not disappoint, laughter is hard to come by unless,
You find the humor in yourself, which is there, and we need to tap. So, laugh, silly, recklessly, tickly, somberly laughter. Does that exist? Yes, I'm losing it laughter is on the edge; the "I'm done laughter.
So, be specific.
I've had enough, I', over the edge, mad scientist laughter is not a frequent but familiar laughter, a compensation a release from the tension of disappointment, or constant unrelenting absurdity of a situation, don't pretend to not know that laughter. It can start as a small growl, or like a hiccup, or a gurgle, but you know it, then you snap out of it and reconsider what you can do instead that is constructive. Like right now. Ha, ha.
Nuyorican Cafe Prompt: Laughter

Part Two

S'AINT (THE EPISTLE ACCORDING TO S'AINT TANESHA)

Grace

A light that shone in-spite of fear, a moment respite from anger, or torture.
A breath, a chance to breathe in and out at one's leisure, is grace.
Oh, sense and acknowledge the soft winded sounding of my lungs forcing air over my nostril hairs, is mindfulness grace provoking, provoking, reminding me to aspire and seek Grace.
The moment of rest and reprieve, the sanctity of long friendships that test limits of patience because they have none, is grace.
The bellows that soften when you are around, the safety, one feels without a sound.
The knowing I want to stay within you, and you round me, is grace.
Oh, the joy in the moment amid confusion grace.
Grace, I want to keep you.
Grace tethers me to silent trust, new possibilities and the sanity of the moment.
A moment of grace is finite and infinite in my hopes that grace never leaves me.
Grace is an aspiration that turns me into an inspiration as it fuels me towards you, I hope with goodness.
Grace is hypnotic only if I allow her, and I need to more often seek her, I hope she will bless me with her presence more.

God loves Black people differently than others. God loves Black people as His special people, and unequal to Europeans overall. Understand that God loves unequally and can because he doesn't say anywhere that He has to love equally. In fact, God is quite subjective in His favors and blessings. Why not? What is not to love when we're made for several purposes!

Yes, God loves us forever unquestionably and yet comparatively. God loves all and some qualitatively more than others. People always say that God is in charge. God is in charge, no doubt. So why expect anything differently? How many ways does God have to explain His world and His intentions for you? He loves you one-way and others another.

It's not a secret. Keep working on being the special person you are. Believe in yourself. Once in a while an exception is planned to be a distraction, someone you're told to aspire to … not really. A test of faith/ label it anyway you want, it's still a truth.

God loves selectively but loves. God denies others on the premise of making one stronger. God plays favorites: He always has, and His consistency is legendary.

So while you wonder and pray, your prayers are answered, within the limits of the category you're assigned, because God rules. Do you have free will? Yes, within the parameters of your station. A few are selected by God to keep you believing otherwise. The Gift is you are on the side that is preferred, and the strength comes from those others.

You are one and the same, both sides considering the perspective He wishes others to perceive.

No one envies strength. Ah yes, you're stronger now, and spent (unless He says you're not of course.) and have been humbled (maybe not quite enough probably), but now broken and humbled (still not good enough). And why? Because God loves you so much that you have the privilege of being beaten again, over, and over. Be forever grateful.

You know how much God loves family and health and sincerity and friendship. God loves everybody. He loves the ones he abuses because He it's His way by reminding us of who is in charge. And the inequities, ah yes, the crafty, dishonest, the liars the bribery mongers, fornicators, adulterers, etc, don't concern yourself with any suffering they might incur sooner, later, or never. He forgives them. And strength, well you can thank God that you earned strength and this understanding. Knowledge and suffering has afforded you comfort and grace. Remember this blessing.

Yes, the stress, the premature ageing, the worry, just learn to give it to God, the one who forecast this in the first place by making you who you are and them the way they are.

He knows how much shorter your life will be from sleepless nights. Your face, worn reflecting the fatigue of mental bruising and the underlying damage to your vital organs. But go to Him. He loves you unequivocally. He loves you. Remember, to love more or less there has to be a relative measurement to that love.

Health, wealth, family, but foremost first Him is all should encompass your life, mind, soul, and being. Be consumed with His glory and omnipotence. Rightfully, rightfully so is the awesome power He commands!

He giveth and He taketh away. He decides, He torments, He loves, and abuses love. He gives you what you need. He takes what he wants. You are fleeting. You are only significant as an example; as a test your role is prescribed. You're a testament of His love no matter what you do and loved deeply for being so. Your replacement is already in a womb!

You're a gift for someone else to open, to compare, hug and stomp. He decided that eventuality. He loves you either way. The other secret is that there is no one to tell Him to put away His toys. Amen.

Fiction

I Cannot Fly Without My Soul To Guide Me

I cannot fly without my soul to guide me.
        My history of journeying
                resides within my soul.
        I soar within landscapes,
        configured for my growth
        my wisdom building.
I land on terrain,
        at first foreign
                then friendly.
I cannot fly without my soul
because my landings are always
airborne, light, at least
Some elemental gas or
Liquid- because if I
drown it's only temporary.
My soul is my thought
preserver, my sense of
Belonging somewhere and
Everywhere as all
journey's are.
So, I fly with my
Soul whether scared or
Shy, bemused or desperate.
BTL Prompt

The Cost, Price, Expense of Hope

It is a lonely, insular road
It is filled with others
Believing there's a chance
What is chance? Chance.
Chance.

Hope is a lonely, insular path
Embellishments from outside
Don't help. Meaning well, sometimes, sometimes
They clutter reality

Hope is a reality. Chance is a
Reality, so why clutter with noise.

Hope is a lonely, insular path
It is an individual's journey because
The unpredictable nature of its
Outcome is unknown and fraught
With uncertainty. Doing all that
Is good is no guarantee.
Then the clutter begins. Well
Meaning clutter. Distilled clutter, spend
Your cost if you still can because the
Cost of hope is high. Lifetime
high.

I needn't find what I did not lose.
Instead, this is a case of remembering and utilizing what I was given.
I found / remembered a fast-tracked use for prayer more essential than before.
I found / remembered a fast-tracked gratefulness for reliable, genuine friends, more crucial than before.
I found / remembered an immediate use for discernment more relevant than before.
I found / remembered an immediate love and utility for having limited patience.
I found / remembered an insightful use for decision making that was always under my control anyway and remembered what's not seemingly in my control, I can alter various ways to meet my future passionately head-on.
I found lessons in every aspect of my life, and I LOVE FINDING avenues never explored before because THE EXCITEMENT OF THE FINDING, the seeking, the presently unknown becomes… KNOWN.

So, what are losses? Losses are holding places for the temporarily un-remembered or newly acquired, newly FOUND TRUTH. Valuable, essential lessons I'll never lose, but keep, and REMEMBER to utilize until I die.
Kemlyn Tan Bappe's Between The Lines (BTL) poet Julian Matthews provided the prompt: Lost and Found

Baskets

Baskets, curved and sweet to the touch and rounded without giving away any other contours; enjoyment and purpose was assured. No one could tell any different today or now in their presence. A coolness that was welcomed no matter the time of day or the mesmerizing feel of the surface becomes repetitive and could be mistaken for soothing. Unblemished to behold and constant, no deviation to contour, capable of sweating, moved by the tactile sense to burst if pressured, and yield a bit if necessary, and almost imperceptibly.

Relatives were also close by and capable of exhibiting several moods and nuances, and all from the same tree which was very obvious. From that same stem so pliant, yet strong, holding the family's sinews, we weave lives together. You call some acquaintances? A few are friends.

Oh yes, baskets get warped, areas are mended, areas become overly worn, areas get taped, areas get strengthened, other areas are left to thinness, and some areas are barely touched, because of… what?

We weave into each other and attract and repel and buoy each other and stack each other, and some can float and some have handles, and some are plaited and decorated and some are undeniably plastic, some are sacred palm, others are recyclable, others not so much.

How do you "weave and bob' bend and fold, press and caress when finding a young green shoot you can frame into your likeness?

Certainly, Lord You See Side By Side Our Outstretched Hands

I live and breathe. I work and toil.
Yet my voice remains out of your laws. You cannot deny me my right to vote. Though you've tried with whip, dogs, and old white men's' hopes. So, I continue to Protest, Organize, and Strategize.
Certainly, Lord you see side by side our outstretched hands.
I work well with neighbors.
I raise fine, strong healthy sons and daughters. We strive for the good of all peoples and yet we are "the enemy." We pay taxes, survive racist wages and still you wonder why I keep my smiling gaze. I see beyond to a greater dawn. My heaven is assured despite you.
So, I continue Protest, Organize and Strategize in plain sight every day, and you're scared of me, I'm not afraid of you.
Certainly, Lord you see side by side our outstretched hands.
I will continue to grow bold and use your lies against you. Keep my mind and my heart on what I know is true. There is no reward until this fight for our votes long overdue is secured legislatively and fully constitutionally in-tune. We'll continue to vote in our Congress and Senate for true fighters our strongest defender. Our voting cause is no light venture. Our futures need securing, without lie, debt or on credit. Our honest actions need no penance.
Certainly Lord you see side by side our outstretched hands.
Non-Fiction: Poet Theresa Davis introduced Dr Doris Derby and her photography during a "Java Speaks" session. This one of several ekphrastic responses I was honored to write.

G-R-A-T-E FUL VERSUS GREATFUL

DO YOU KNOW WHAT IS SHREDDED BEYOND RECOGNITION IN ORDER TO BE GREATFUL?
DO YOU KNOW WHAT IS BULLY FORFEITED IN ORDER TO DEMAND GREATFUL-NESS?
DO YOU KNOW WHY THE TERM IS BANTERED BY MANY AND PRACTISED BY SO FEW?
G-R-A-T-E IS A PULVERIZATION, DISSECTION OF A MASS DOWN SOMETIMES TO A GRINDING DUST.
YOU ARE FUEL OF THE GRATED MATERIAL WHICH HAS LEVELS ON THEIR MACHINE.
THE MENTAL AND PHYSICAL GRATER USED
BLOODILY,
EFFORTLESSLY,
GENERATIONALLY PASSED DOWN IN THEIR RECIPE BOOKS
"ADD SPITE,
ADD A DOLOP OF VENOM,
A SPRINKLING OF INSECURITY MIXED THROUGHOUT,
THEN GRATE THE BLOCK OF HUMANITY,
GRATE AND REDISTRIBUTE EVENLY ACROSS THE PAN SHEET.
DON'T LET IT RISE,
JUST ROLL OVER IT UNTIL STICKINESS EVAPORATES.
WATER IT TEMPTINGLY, A FEW DROPS
AND WHEN HARDENED
ROLL IT SOME MORE WITH YOUR PIN OF JUSTICE AND JAIL AND SCHEME AND LIES AND FALSEHOODS.
BAKE ON THE SAME TEMPERATURE YOU BAKE YOUR THOUGHTS OVER COOL COCKTAILS AND POLITICAL POWER YATCH AND GOLF MEETINGS.
SLICE, PLATE, CONSUME. REPEAT RECIPE WHILE THE ---?

Oh yes, that massive block you saved from extinction you say REMAINS GREATFUL TO WHOM?

"Younger LOVES Barley Bread Now"

After the festivities died down and father extended the "honey, period" of course during this entire time I continued working, as expected, and as usual.

Told to get over my angst, stop behaving badly and accept this as a learning lesson leaning on my forgiveness threshold.
I swallowed my pride, ate grain not lamb chops, FED the live-stock, tended the field, paid wages, fixed fences, bayed at the ,, clipped my toenails by ,light since lamp oil is expensive and we have to help Younger regain his footing, because "God forbid he stumble in a field on pebbles or sharp stones bleeding his delicate toes and uncalloused heels!

But I digress.

Soon, the loafing began, but actually never ended. Amnesia "on how to do anything" reappeared. Does this sound familiar to anyone?
"Deaf father," has continuing excuses. "Give him time to get his bearings."
What bearings? Never had any, wasn't interested, and guess what... still isn't.
That's what happens when you reward, …wait for it… sloth and ingratitude.

I wouldn't know what those are. I just live here.

Oh, leaving everything to me father? Really?

Younger's not pulling his weight and has no intention it seems. When father dies, as the good fool I am, I will not let Younger live as a destitute because the eldest is always the fool. the good fool. The faithful fool, the loyal to parents caring fool the fool with a conscious and the Youngster will get over. one who reaps so much from doing so little.

News for you? I don't forget. I will remind others far and wide what an ungrateful wretch is, and everyone sees uncaring to boot, for the motivation to return to us was not from yearning for family, there was no burning bush, no prophet readings, no dreams of a heartbroken and worried father, no, Younger's motivation was clear.

Younger's belly bellowed, not the voice of God.
Younger heard the voice of his belly, not the voice of God.
The growl of the empty gut, not the voice of God. Not the pain of an empty heart.

Younger felt the spasm and smelled expulsion of gut gas not the voice of God, not God, not homesickness, not " I am sorry and need to work for a change." Younger's belly ruled Younger's actions, so others will follow Youngers example especially if they have a father like ours unless I provide the full narrative.

No scowling father! Younger has to earn chow! Better now than never. Growling stomachs not Youngster's better
No justice, no relief, no justice, no work relief, no work relief, no chore relief. Think I am just running this place so Youngster can eat sheep!

Now father is gone. No chore relief. Younger gets no beef. Justice finally takes a seat.

Younger loves eating barley bread and porridge now. My friends and I are having a killer BBQ as our chow.
I'll sit back and watch. Younger finally blisters hands and toes from handling trowel, spade and plows.

Sweet. I need a toothpick and sit back now resting my back and feet.

Grateful for simple threads and adequate power, ever busy for us as siblings to satisfy our heritage, upkeeps and needs, He has no time for selfish deeds. No heavenly scowl will I receive upon Pearly Gates well pleased. Sometimes lessons can go afoul unless they are tempered with sound, wise love and adult actions are found.

Younger and I will resume as siblings and as fitting examples, generations willing.

EctEtc Example

Stillness

Hi I'm Stillness.
I'm part of you, and easy on the eye. I did that purposely. I'm not an enemy. I'm like a great sauce ingredient, I'm in there!
I'm a great conversationalist if you let me! No judgement, just exchange. Occasionally, I raise my hand. I know you see me on your fringe peripheral vision, mind's eye. You pretend that I'm not part of you.
Some people seem afraid of me, Stillness.
Some people are afraid of quiet.
Some peopled are reticent to listen to their own thoughts.
They tell me, Stillness, invites inquiry, paying attention to demons left unsaid and left to lie in murky waters one doesn't wish to stir…perhaps.
When don't I bring solace or peace, or closeness to love, and instead invite dread, moroseness, fear, battles, lost fights, bruising?
How does one change me, Stillness to a synonym for constructive silence, mending, comfort, joy, and happy anticipation?
You find the words to write from me in your moments of engagement with me when you allow my release you welcome my spirit when you need to find the right word *mot. N'est pas?*
Bon. We both only remember high school French so don't get carried away.
I use the word and concept *stillness* in many of my poetic works.
I love myself. Stillness.
If you know how to change me into constructive meditation, or mind meanderings without pressure, and labeling teach it, use yourself as an example of my healing powers.
Start with loving yourself.
I am Stillness. I am not your enemy. It is balm, it is you the beautiful person you are, we all are despite several faults, trying to speak and saying hi, I hurt too.

Hi, this thought is overdue. Hi, let's take steps together. Hi, my name is Stillness, nice to meet you. I have no hidden agendas; you already know what we're about!
Hi, I am your friend and I'll never leave you. I'm you. Let's dialogue without blame, just as forever loving friends.
Remember, I'm a great conversationalist if you let me! No judgement, just exchange. Occasionally, I raise my hand. I know you see me on your fringe peripheral vision, mind's eye. You pretend that I'm not part of you, but I am. I don't cost anything, just ring me up.
A Benicia Inspiration

The Pieta Twice Beheld Her

The Pieta twice beheld her in its marble grasp.
Taken from her breast and thigh beheld them both in mind and spirit both too young to recognize the legacy they left behind to mother, friend, relative, and child.
Friends of the family may arise and linger but for awhile.
Through seasons this never changes for both lives beheld their mother sainted.
She drew them both and gave them hope in a world devoid of a lasting scope.
Bearing ever that pyre of burning desire to hold and hear them again.
Release, release, and teach us my dear, for you of His greatest makes you revered.
Non-Fiction

Lasting Memories, Radiant Hope

Do you recall the smell of soaps and cologne elders wore? Do you recall holiday kitchen smells? Weekday kitchen smells? Do you recall the lotion we all used to soften our skin and look dewy? Because the television announcer convinced us that we did and our eyes glazed over and began to believe it, so we are convinced that this stuff is good, look it works.

Suddenly our eyes soften, and the gaze seems more forgiving, our creases disappear because we have radiant hope. It was the addition of beets juice and drinking more water and having a more positive outlook and getting rid of verbal assailants quicker and reminding you of your mortality to say what you must now not later.

My radiant hope I personify in my body and my deeds and hopefully as I remember the smells of lotions and soaps and comforting food, I build a lasting memory for someone else.

Non-Fiction: Benicia Prompt

Get Up, You're Embarrassing Our Pew

I have a confession to make, I fake out people who don't come to church regularly.

I kind of pray that maybe if I confess to you my church siblings, I can be truly good and completely remorseful.

I pretend to kneel when it's time to sit and pretend to sit when it's time to kneel.

The "Holiday Holies" provide particularly easy fodder for my transgression. I should not judge their air of snobbery. I should not presume excessively generous generational tithing and stock market treasures upon the death of their patriarchs and matriarchs is guaranteed in wills to the church.

I've gone to confession twice about this, but now I have stopped, being bad that is. The inner chuckle I admit to you I still feel, isn't as strong as it used to be. Part of me wants to write, darn it, penance almost worked! The holy part of me admits "That's religious progress." Okay. Yes. No trumpets?

I guess this explains why my paperwork for sainthood is on hold. Darn it. I confess, I'm worried. Let's face it, the more time I get provides additional presenting opportunities for me to screw-up. Consistency of nature, and good will are important saintly qualities. I believe I should get credit that my inner chuckle dies a little more when I remember these crucial requirements for sainthood.

It's safe to sit next to me. You better be a regular parishioner from here, oops I almost forgot, or not. I guess that's what temptation is, the ability to confuse the innocent knowingly. How innocent are they really that I have so many to victimize? Did I write victimize? No, I'm not a predator. Not me! Mass is on YouTube; look it up you heathen, I meant fellow-brethren. I almost slipped there. Enjoying the love? There's no saint with my name yet because, well.

You're the only one still kneeling, why is that? Oh, that's

between you and God of course. Not judging. Follow the ushers because you don't know where to turn. Not judging.
The rest of us like the old lady who sacrificed her last three cents as a sacrifice give into baskets. Never saw this before. Oh. Ushers need to wait for you to shuffle an envelope at the last minute out of your purse/breast pocket, because you didn't see them coming up the aisle, really?
I obviously have a long way to go. Darn it. Amen.
Yep, Non-Fiction

Concert

Defined as silent-space walls, in reality this partitioned area serves as an echo chamber recalling whispers. Whispered admonishments, tears, appeals, promises, prayers and more appeals reverberating in many faiths promises occasionally kept. Reverence sometimes comes from silences, telepathic musings, aura connections, electricity and mantra-driven quiet. In such a place you remember inner thoughts. Allowing quiet reawakens these strengths. Man-made screens in multipurpose spaces jumpstart a level of privacy for the mind, and the eye, without blocking pathways to an intended receiver. This area provides reflection and calm without judgement.

Souls and spirits hover in this area, it's a welcoming respite from hospital corridors. Hospital corridors can become busy avenues.-Trafficking incessantly both the newborn and lifeless, hospital corridors carry balloons, these flouncing mini-floats to celebrate birthdays, applaud tests affirming improvements and sometimes for the presumed final viewing of a usually faithful parade fan.

For modesty, screens block patient's partial nudity from unintentional eyes, or from procedures only staff should know are occurring. Screens temporarily partition and exclude; however, any form can be carried away. We can be carried away by unexpected encounters.

He sang from his inner tenor, and I from my inner mezzo-soprano. "For the sake, of his glorious passion …."The Divine Mercy Chaplet at 1:00 PM, I sang monthly within Mt Sinai's Chapel, NYC.

Medical staff would come during their break to recharge, commit to a brief shut-eye, contemplate their day, pray, sit. Honestly, they were always on duty. Sitting is a verb. Slumping is less an active verb and lying down (without snoring) lesser an active sport. Anyway, sometimes staffers would come in; oftentimes I'd be "almost alone"with my intentions and hopes for my patients. My dearly departed friend Faye smiled everytime I sang. This particular afternoon, I was not physically alone.

We were screen separated; which his voice and mine ignored. His voice in Arabic prayer, mine in English prayer. I didn't require a translation because I knew his lingering notes were heartfelt and genuine. I sensed he felt that way about my part of our duet. Un-rehearsed, there was neither interruption nor intermission. The room hummed. My unknown prayer-mate gifted me with a beautiful memory. I hope he left our concert with the same complementary spirit.

Non-Fiction

Carry

Unknown to me how, when, I do not know.
I am different, I didn't know before,
Did I have a clue?
My friends will wonder, with who?
Possessed?
Unknown to me, yet knowing of me
Watched from my inception?
My first crawl, my first footfall. My first bruise, my first tears, recorded?
Watched me at the well, school, home, cooking, with neighbors,my parents rousing at every daybreak and nightfall?
How should I feel but blessed.
Scared, excited, shamed, dreamed, no eavesdroppers during this swoon.
But a witness to my God. So we alone know the truth; no desire so swept away except not with the hand of man but of God.
Be merciful to me as fulfilling every want and need for I know not man, only You.

Yes, You Fulfilled Your Purpose, Now Watch the Reign

Surely self-gratification graces your brow.
Surely, to know you've succeeded in determining your own demise, well I doubt you can morally grasp this fact. Surely in your role as a recurring catalyst, your ethical sight-line is too dim to fathom repercussions.
Surely, I'll find the time to explain because I'm gracious and filled with compassion. So, as simply as I can let's start with how you and your like-minded peers operate. Look, it's us, so no harm to admitting the obvious about your admirers and fellow ambassadors. You're a sterling transparent example!
Surely some secret glee graces your lip curl when those like me literally and figuratively die.
Surely some molecule hops upon a synapse exuding pleasure, drowsy comfort and self-aggrandizing "Atta-boys" thumbs-up accompanies such accomplishments.
Surely some can't wait to hear the news of your latest conquests.
Surely a parade with fanfare and confetti awaits you with badges felt deservedly conferred and displayed.
Surely confetti you fashioned out of others like me will be spread. Surely some consider shredding others like newspaper print black and white no crime by your kind. Surely no distinction except in your case; since you color-code the shredder, with replacement parts easy to find.
Surely stockpiled for centuries and funded exponentially, your safety and belief in such tyranny was infinitely guaranteed.
Surely, you thought so.
Surely, it's ending.
Surely, you sense it. The self-serving brow, lip curl and comfort are becoming the history of your demise by your own design.
Surely, we already know your centuries old fear. We lick our lips; our heightened synapses are already THERE.
Our parades don't use confetti. We know what you shred.

Worthless our emails proving your guilt, because accountability is only applied on one side, not yours. Our defiance to your emails, and your manipulated defense of half-truth and the unsubstantiated which you leave to us, with convenience loss and non-proofs because they float, airborne and brushed aside and dumped as waste. There is no wasted time. Every effort is worthwhile. Every deliverance a step forward, always and forever. You shred. Those leftovers can stuff your pillows/comforters/duvets, while reminiscing and drugging yourself to sleep. The nightmares you'll self-induce.

Moving forward, we'll tell you where you're allowed to gawk, sit and squirm. Grasp hands with your replacement parts, sing of the good old days you had while we reassign/realign/redistribute you.

Surely some we'll bind like crumbled newspaper print and transport some up to the information laden "Cloud" locked-down and either abandon, keep disoriented, or help them self-suffocate.

Surely you recall the choices those like me were given.

Surely you fulfilled your purpose. Lessons learned, oh yes for some, not all, for some not ever. Save a few? Maybe. But in the now, surely some gratification.

Watch the Reign

There is no need to feign indignation or to pretend stupefied, when your ill-gotten gains whether exposed now or after are revealed. Those stalwart ones you paid into silence, is the same as slavery. How many pretenders have been bought, but really, who cares? There's always a market recycled thought, recycled wealthy, recycled deliberate abuse, and attempts to define someone else. You don't write that script. Who's the fool? Who's not actualized to their full potential? You cannot imagine!

How convenient we should work together, when you are at a loss, when your own are susceptible, when your own are gassed? How convenient when you've had to shelter? Here's a good excuse to come out, call it a cause. How sincerely do you

feel anything? Look you up in ten – fifteen years. Still stalwart, non -conformist? Still the caring of the majority because, who's the minority? Afraid of the ethnically, and genetically rainbowed majority?
Watch the Reign
Alive in your cocoon so safe, it takes an unseen force to disturb your slumber. What do you hide behind? How many falsify who they are to get ahead? Laugh at on-color jokes? Smirk like EEO tells you not to? But you will see to it so you forfeit decency and fairness and delude yourself by reimagining it as "teamwork".
Watch the Reign
Clouds are white for a reason all year round. Some turn gray and then considered threatening, for a reason. Gray is the color of wisdom. Dark is foreboding in their language for a reason. Jesus is white in many households for a reason. Then suddenly, oh color doesn't matter. Oh yeah, but you've proven color matters to you, oh hypocrite. So, who looks the closest to a savior? One that's been burnt or used sunscreen in the desert? No great master in the colonist power are praising black, brown saviors, except one who knows the truth. God must look like your cousin or Mary like you mother or the lady in your village with as many vowel-ed surnames as possible.
Watch the Reign
Atmospheric pressure is a…what? Storms are a....what? Lightening is yellow. Sky is colored too. Sunset is shades of …. what? Sunrise, yes. Don't trip on our robes, just Watch the Reign.
Non-Fiction

So, This Is Love?

Where has the time gone?
Time is irrelevant when
I'm with you.
It's sooooo true.
I didn't believe that
time flies by. But
it does when I'm
with you.
We were both still
young-ish when we
Met.
Then we became mature-ish
Now we're more mature-ish
I didn't believe that
Time flies by, but it
Does when I'm with you.
I wear an eight now.
Not a five-six.
We still have dimples
Mine are in places
I can't fix.
It doesn't matter though.
So, this is love?
Non-Fiction: Prompt provided by Daryl Fun

"I Am…"
No, I'm not Pocahontas. No, I am not Hiawatha, no I'm not Sacajawea,
I'm Mrs. Tonto.
I don't see anyone dressed like me for Halloween.
Behind every great man is an outstanding woman!
He looks good, right? Those deerskins don't fit themselves you know.
Funny, you can pronounce every basketball, football, tennis players names with long letters but our family names you have a problem pronouncing so you use a short version you can both spell and pronounce, "Tonto." Just saying.
We know, Tonto means fool.
R: Oh, you want to say something, sure …

****

Yes, I am Pura Belpré.
I was the first Puerto Rican Librarian hired by the New York City Public Library.
I don't see anyone dressed like me for Halloween.
Our oral traditional folk tales need to be documented in books for all Hispanic children to know and read and love. Encouraging books and printed materials with our stories for future generations reference and use. It's important for our children to know, have, be proud of their heritage and these treasures would otherwise disappear when elders are no longer here.
A favorite romantic tale Perez (the Mouse) and Martina (Spanish Cockroach) is but one example of our strong heritage folk tales.
CUNY Hunter College has an entire "biblioteque" of my films, books, and tapes.
R

****

Recognize me? Yes, I am Mary Magdalene.
Yes, I am an apostle.
No, he doesn't have blue eyes and blond hair, look at where we've from.
I continue to pray for you ... some of you don't have a prayer, anyway. you John, Matthew, Paul, James, they all say "you know you look just like Mrs. Tonto. well, you know why of course. oh, do want to say something of course, keep prayerful
R

****

I am Kalpana Chawla the first Indian American woman astronaut to go into space.
I don't see anyone dressed like me for Halloween.
Unfortunately, I died in the space shuttle Columbia disintegration in 2003.
I hope I remain an inspiration to boys and girls still.
Oh, the stars these universes, the immensity. Absolutely amazing. Continue to explore and reach further and further out into this vast space.
Oh, would you like to speak to them? Of course ...
R

****

I am RBG
Now this is truly the Supreme, Supreme Court.
Very bright here. Yes, I'm Ruth Bader Ginsburg.
I don't see anyone dressed like me for Halloween. Oh no, I see a few.
We still have lots of work to do. I'm still with you. I'm working

from here. I see you still trying. Don't give up, we still have lots of work to do.
If I had four sons one of them, I would use her maiden name for the first name of one of them, (our people do that you know).
R

****

Yes of course. Come captive audience…
I am Diane Murray Ward. On behalf of Mrs. Tonto, Pura Belpré, Mary Magdalene, Kalpana Chawla, and Ruth Bader Ginsberg guess what? We're all the same. Thank you.
Non-Fiction: Performed for hybrid Paris/New York event for Nuyorican Café

Wombworth

How many new soldiers can you provide for men?

We don't discriminate too much.

Send us your sons and daughters.

We don't discriminate, too much

Soldier up, soldier down, we don't mind your periodic menses too much, anymore.

An ability to fight and take direction, silent sighing, whimpering from all the genders, don't care too much anymore.

How many new soldiers can you provide for men?

Most with wombs would rather bargain, perhaps, don't assume for that would be a mistake.

Womb holders can be just as treacherous, ego vampires sucking their juices from wherever they can…so just remember and let's get to the point

How many new soldiers can you provide for men?

Almost sounds like a choice, right?

Tired of what seems like busywork, new patterns of 'put-off and wait some more" crafts, listening through their faulty ear, postponing unnatural deaths you accelerate to help, and all the cookie cutters wombs can hold just as long as you can birth soldiers provided for men.

While you are commerce-d for your labor rarely tallied, you have no time to dally, You soldier up, soldier down, fields, canneries, sweatshops, grain-ery. seashores, every nook and cranny for food sustenance, and the wheel of homespun, nameless in labors of both types, basketed awaiting your loin-dropped expecting to full suckle on your exhausted frame,

new soldiers for men.

Apparently, some men were not crystalized first in wombs, but raised forfeiting others their opportunities to rise in equality.

Apparently, politics frame some mothers' hips

Determining what's best for her nation's future is the additional labor role placing both she and her babies at risk

Poking in any fertile field, men don't discriminate if it's soldiers they need.

Muted by the blasts, their wives and daughters safely set aside. Teaching them to raise only those bred to order and profit somehow in all the ways war benefits are designed. Blast and rebuild, wound and become a hospital guild, war has benefits mortar, plaster backroom cast, heatseeking drones drop food, medicines and possibly blaster sealing caps.

The personhood with those who provide the blood and guts of the marginalized only good enough to strut flags and leave their teeth, return if "lucky?" less a spleen, bury their bone parts in lands where men of war surf.

"Almost terribly sorry" for your loss, but you're still young, "bear-able" and have ample, nice, full beauty spots. So, tell me, how many new soldiers can you provide for men?

Gather data, quantify, keep you busy, commute, commune and smile. Can I sit at the big table yet, please? Stilettos, falsettos, comfortable pumps have no place in the damming deal. We can entertain calmly and compromise at the sanity not vanity table.

Work and work and scan the globe, have you enhance your segregated title, labeled and staffed roles, and carry on, fearlessly charting the woes of women. Womb holders labor pains otherwise forgotten and build and concretize what men of war all too well already know, who still believe a pat on the head is sufficient setback for our political power accountability, and enforcement needs woes.

Since we're talking, while you're here how many soldiers can you provide for the war's needs? So, noted.

Inspired as NGO/CSW volunteer/attendee

In the Birth Canal of Death

In the Birth Canal of Death losers gamble that their finality would end with a win.

There isn't any reckoning, just tempered equality.

There is no sweetness to stench, we all putrefy.

We are all elemental and water.

No dust, no ash appears any different, or does it?

Are saviors granular? Are the wicked globules? Are the brusk pebbly?

Are the meek evaporate and light?

Can you mix them in urns when they wouldn't mix in life?

What chemistry happens in the birth canal of death; anything preparatory? Is it just the disengagement of molecules to build souls of others, or do you become part of a cucumber, or bird seed, or the bird or a leaf, or the song in a whale's throat?

Do you sense who you were before by the glimpse of a scarf you recognize now worn around the neck of a pet goat about to be slaughtered?

In the birth canal of death, you are not patted to breathe, your last breath is already payment, the coinage forfeited, the cost of your next "cruise."

The birth canal of death is your end as known now, just a wink, a blotch, a carbon dot, a mess, a foe, a friend, a love. You didn't decide who would love you. You came to experience absurdities, injustices, madness, and the cruelty inflicted. You came to experience the difference between like and love and lust and "Do not stalk." Do I have to repeat that last one?

Now, payment for wrongdoings is payment reduced to ash.

There is no justice for all even when in the last nanosecond to actually feel anything resembling warmth, love, truth, while searing heat scorches some. Too late is their last gulp for the one time in their existence an attempt to sound sincere with no one to hear them say "I'm sorry" or knowingly still pompous and ready to return just (choose one or all that apply) as racist, or ego-centric, all defaulting, or too dangerous for humanity as before, this "utterance" resounds where ? By whom? Counts towards…?

Forged stronger and tempered within the birth canal of death are two types. The scared, fever-pitched, revengeful, insecure versus the ever-innocent hunted upon prey. The prey prays.

One colossal game. Weighted, scored, reshuffled, and rehearsed. Rules change for one side, intended to assess the dedication, creativity, and resilience of the other. This is not at all mystifying. Viewers watch amused and pay for more. The birth canal of death is a major slot machine with rigged chances. Don't be surprised. We are truly woven with universal elements from the same extra-terrestrial gene pool. We share an inheritance of twisted sensibilities wired anciently; after-all we too still pay for entertainment of all sorts.

The Arks

I don't need Europeans
to tell me I am
from the stars. For I am their elder and they are failing yet again. Some have a passing grade this time, but not barely enough to consider as appreciably significant to calibrated change.
Their denial is futile though taking them years if ever to acknowledge their acceptance remains irrelevant. They cry within their crucible of requiring for themselves "tangible proof," Ha, Such simpletons! (I'm using "non-naughty" language in case this is one day allowed in a classroom of those under 50 years old.)
To convince you of how disposable you are, yet valuable at the same time, I have left structures in the sea, at depths where we lab and quantify your
(I use the word loosely) "development." Let's face it the "Sands of time" are not in your favor yet again! Pix axes and trowels! Good luck with that! Ha!
Survey transits providing vertical and horizontal, and leaf trowels, using plumb bobs and sieves to find me . It's the only time you kneel before me on foam your mats and spades of metal your shaker screens now value every minute piece of me. You're looking backwards.
In the same way they are wont to say "Moving forward" in their rude way when they are challenged with a task, they were to perform but renege because you told them to do it. As expected by the insecure trying to gain prominence. The stakes are still too immense for their cognitive intake
I HAVE BEEN LEAVING YOU CLUES.
Their justification is for their own immoral thinking and false needless and imagined sense of a moral based pride.
Who is the one with unequal thoughts, with devious intent from

bully religion for bully faith for bully killing to justify their beliefs?

We never forced you to change your languages, We never forced you to act our sustaining bread or obey our soil, land, animals. But we fed you so you could gain the traitors strength you still have, because loyalty to you has always had a price and power tag. Afraid we may enslave you in the future? Well, you're in for big "Whoop!"

You destroy what you do not own, you destroy what you cannot conquer and infer your yoke of false hood. You preach faith and spirit, yet you quench with poisonous urine that hisses out of you onto pureness. You hate the smoke rising, because the ash reflects your false hubris in believing the lies you tell yourself. You wreck our bodies with diseases our plants did not know how to fend off, immediately, so we died. What diseases have we given you? The contagion of helping you survive this country, new to you, not us.

The contagion was your spirit, your greed, your dismissal of our land, culture by torture and deceit.

You have not paid in full yet.

Your harm is without a monetary figure. The cost of lives is immeasurable, and you still don't care.

So, the arks will return. The experiment is ongoing. Just so you know, I humbly submit that I haven't failed the test because to fail the test would be to ignore what you've done, and I cannot in all honest truth let that remain unsaid. Let me explain in a way you'll understand because, your moral, ethical, sustainable neurons remain inactivated; still self-change nutrient strength, still below par.

Let's pick examples you can relate to, I did not pollute your water, I did not steal your homes with exorbitant mortgage rates based on race, I did not strangle your elders, I did not rape, abuse, force into servitude any of you. I did not starve you but breastfed your babies. I did not covet your children I didn't steal your wages, give false testimony in court because "someone's got to pay for the curious demise of your own and it might as well be one mine off the street, which helps your cause of killing blackbirds / brown birds / yellowbirds, redbirds with one sacrificial stone. Did I hear you gasp? Just fooling, we've experienced you clutching your bags in elevators when others step in trying to ascend other floors so many times that your reflex is "old norm," we're so familiar with your automatic drill. By the way European kids steal purses too, they don't get any jail time, records get expunged, and "He's really a GOOD boy, had POTENTIAL, BOYS WILL BE BOYS,etc. Also, since we all look alike, he was probably time for you to get caught on something, since we didn't catch you doing something else, right?

I did not try to even think about annihilating you until you showed your true colors.

So, as they are astonished by findings I left them, in the sea and under the sands, when we knew they were not ready before and continue to cause their own undoing, I realize some of us have been tempted by the same faults that cause the world such pain and discomfort, so the arks will return yet again. Pain will ensue, yet again, exploration will continue, yet again, love and peace will remain elusive yet again, and each time lessons will be slowly gained and lost, your memories erased to appoint, until you truly learn that the best comes from cooperation, but you are slow to slow comparable y to other species. Time for you will end and when you become "cog proof" because myth is too hard for you to accept, so brown knows nothing till you have something in your hands.

Not for us. You have not changed European. Too late for some, not all. I have a list somewhere, don't worry, I have it nearby. You're a strain (Get it?) we knew would provide a curious change to the nutrient base.

Our cultures truths you readily dismissed without

Do you consider this corralling? Do you consider this branding? Do you consider this umbrellaing? When you negatively set -up someone and I call it "whitemailing" you always tense up.

Having Black Friday is a start I guess in your headset. So, instead you resort to "dark times phraseology." Is that dark white, or is dark just the opposite of white which can't be good, right? Or am I conditioned navy?

No, some of you just think you're so bright in your snobbery and racism. Just so you know, there's no front of the ark and back of the ark, no reserved seating, no upper deck, lower deck, no prime tickets, please ask me about season tickets, cause you all only have the season you'll know is when I let you off on land again! Gulp.

You'll mixed because of fear, And since I'm at the helm, anyone acting will be thrown overboard because their passage has no continent until I drop you off where I think you need to be to learn all over, for your souls to learn maybe you need to be a native this time around to get a feel of what you do as a European and vice versa.

Don't mind me, do your thing.

Where am I? Thanks to you. I'm great! I am in the company pool, placing bets on you. I 'm taking notes all the time, and my peers and I, see you.

Marrow

When headaches plague, and threaten teetering blindness
I either acknowledge pollen the culprit or promise to clean filters for
I am intimately familiar with being too tired to dust.

When a roaring sound overtakes my ears and everyone nearby hears
I either acknowledge or look straight ahead for
I am intimately familiar with its source.

When limbs seem to fumble, and my mobility's challenged function is noticed
I either acknowledge tripping or pretend that "muscles fell asleep" for
I am intimately familiar with its cause.

When irritability rages and becomes my response to a callus world
I either acknowledge your intentional ignorance of my circumstance or swallow excuses that your center stage is fully booked for
I am intimately familiar with such scheduling.

When I can't make enough saliva to taste "What's That Soup?"
I either acknowledge that the weather isn't numbing cold or I haven't enough self-generated heat to ward off diseases I am more susceptible to succumb to
I am intimately familiar with such gnawing

When sleep disallows dreaming and screaming hasn't any strength because knowledge of diminishing reserves rarely has an outlet.

When sound becomes bold and my knocking knees can't my body hold.
When you know I need yet withhold, I taste the marrow of my bones. DMW

Fiction, thank God.
May 2025 submission for the Poetry X Hunger platform provided by Hiram Larew

Shudder

I felt as if I knew her and

was familiar

with that look.

It's a universal

sensibility.

Thank you, Dominique.

Ekphrastic response to Dominique Dève's artwork appearing in "RATTLE"

Moonbound? Who Invited You?

My name is Diane, aka Artemis.

Yeah, Goddess of THE MOON!

I would invite you, but I've seen

what you've done to the earth

So, stay home!

When you learn manners

I might let you have a trial

stayover, otherwise

stay home!

Brats like you don't respect your homes

I don't assume you'll respect mine

(i.e. Planting flags, dirt rovers leaving tracks, who does that? You do!)

I'll notify you if I want you to visit

You already pollute space with

A plethora of debris, ahhh

You know what…

stay home!

Caitlin and Jacob Jans host an annual twenty-four hour poetry marathon. The twenty-fourth hour prompt was: Write a poem that contains the word "moonbound."

Part Three

MUSE NOURISHMENT

Soul Source

A garden at night is still beautiful and effuses its fragrance from the heat of the day. So did she.

Driven to this apartment by their confidant, she enters a forgotten world when time was savored. A lethargic, palm-fronded fan whirred overhead. A bowl over-laden with fragrant lemons and peaches shares a tiny table's space beside a hurricane-stylized lamp. Its' fluted top is covered by a rose-hued hanker-chief.

An accompanying table held crystal goblets and various sized bottles containing liquids clear, rose and deep clarets.

A fusion of mangoes and wild greens salad, two casserole dishes, one filled with sweet potato bread, and coconut scones, and yet another with chilled raspberries and mint leaves appeared on another table. Centered was the bouillabaisse; kept warm by the single candle, almost unnoticeable, heating the chafing dish's underbelly.

The driver left her standing in the middle of the room looking out onto the darkness above the garden.

The cushioned loveseat faced the wrought iron, filigreed glass balcony doors. Its white shirred curtains opened wide to accept the garden's breeze. A light rain began that patterned the syncopation of the fan.

The misted breeze played with errant wisps of hair that framed her face and draped down her shoulders. It lingered across her nostrils so that she could smell garden roses, lilacs, the room's seafood and peaches.

Her immersion was almost complete.

Then, one waivering breeze hummed between her nape warmer than the surrounding air; it's residue too moist to be dew, and it's source too fleshy to be cloudlike.

Sliding across her belly, his hand encircled her waist. She tried to swallow imperceptibly. He faced her.
She felt his eyelashes flutter against her as he licked her solar plexus.
There was no breeze when she became his wind.

My Muse Doesn't Nap

Where there is a thought to be registered, notes become their voice
And I sing within
When there are thoughts to be considered
Notes become their voice and I write
Where are thoughts that do not want to disappears again, my voice attempts to imitate their sensory feel
Non-Fiction

If I Were a Book, Would I Be Banned?

If I were a book, would I be banned? Of course, I'd be banned,
not at first, but eventually.
I would couch my comments in a lullaby, a swing -a-bye or three
blind rodents, almost any kiddie song, because mine enemy isn't
bright.
Of course, I'd be banned, not at first, but eventually the audio
book would follow the melody of a collage of favorite American
toons thus far allowed and not yet (un?) sanctioned.
Of course, I'd be banned, not at first, but eventually because I
wouldn't sing it. I'd be a marked, masked singer, wear gloves,
and utilize a voice change attachment so that you couldn't tell
it's me even upon my speaking voice.
Of course, I'd be banned, not at first, but eventually because my
"nom de plume" would be divulged by angry someone I trusted
who could be bought off with a flight ticket to the , and I don't
mean piloted by Ralph via Kramden Airlines!
Of course, I'd be banned, because I'm not going to change, just
the circumstances allowing my free speech taking on another
form.

A prompt inspired by Java Speaks workshop poet Daryl Funn

The Red-Shanked Douc Langur

Not enough of you are missing me yet, although some have noticed.
Like butterflies and fireflies fleeting, also going, going, almost gone but I'm a bit bigger, though some don't seem to be missing me, just yet.
I am free to climb and free to roam with my friends and family high up in the trees,
Where I hurt no-one unless they are leaf or mineral rich dirt field.
I scamper to … where again?
Everyone is "in the know," there are no secrets in this company
We flit about, sometimes use scouts, and so we've learned by looking at you, because now my friends are few and scarce, all because of you, You and YOU!
My beauty doesn't scare anyone, my eyes don't pieces your soul.
I am different from you in many ways, you've listed all my woes, but somehow you forget to list besides my diet and temperament, how scarce, how violent and how much less of mine there will be because of your humanness.
My value in your medicines, my value perhaps previously for sport, any kindness you once had for me, is truly, utterly lost unless as you count, now how my relatives have dwindled, will become myths in your generation's lineage,
Want to keep me alive? Leave me alone and I'll thrive, because with you I will surely die.
As we die in our canopy homes, perhaps have a few loved on around to reminisce about our past homes, we'll share a few buds, howl a few last high-pitched howls to our beautiful sky, and falling to Mother Earth, upon assuming one last rigid pose, pray that humans stop killing those born like me at birth.

Hunting Innocence

I hid within this marsh-like ground.
Offering depths at different spots quake with offerings differing loose depths to Hades entry.
The reed and I blend, bend more than the russet dusking the skyline
His spider-y, my russet, my mahogany deepened by the beet red tinged juicing my veins that pound my heart above my breast-plate imagined because of his spear sharpened eyes, piercing all darkness, looking for me, lusting for me, craven desire and his love of the hunt.
Treachery tentacles seek me out
With spies? And babies like me seeking me out
awaiting my rich, fragrant nectar for their rewarding.
I hide, quiet and prayerful.
Kneeling floating away to deliverance or to another hell?
The earthly hell made for me in my innocence
Another juicing my veins? Hope from the recurringly capturing, quicksand or open waves to safety, we both offer prayers to decide.
There are ways to silence my gurgling belly and echoing womb.
My ekphrastic response to "Hiding and Waiting" by Henry L. Jones, poet and artist.

Goddess Let's Be Clear Daikus

Let's be clear, you wish. I will never hunt you down. Your wish list is dead.
I'm a goddess, you're…? Yeah, I've known Trojans, a few. None of them like you.
Let's be clear, you wish. Wish upon a star, what world. Flower petals too!
I'm a goddess. You're…? I'm ethereal, you're not. Trust me, I'm way hot.
Drooling, perspiring. You'll end up looking like snot. Mops and bucket team.
Burning with desire, Yes, poet, pap-pee, jailbait. It's called lust you fool.
My beam in your eyes, betray your lying, moist lips, seduction complete.
The need for a pause, allows for strengthening thoughts, cupping lovely dreams.
For all we hold dear, know that time doesn't stand still, you're not still either.
Don't forget your soul, Too late for some there's no doubt, You're saved anyway.
Can't find a spirit, can't double-cross everyone, God is myopic?
Spirals in one's mind, like ringlets causing mazing, and attempts to hide.
Do colors mature? Can rainbows darken alone? Still building storm clouds?
Prayers are shy sometimes. Prayers mean well, usually. Some prayers are questions.
We are metallic. Shimmering and conductive. Ignition differs.
When there is movement, imperceptible at times, watch eye pupils change.
Honesty is rare. Too bad trust is fleeting too, sadly if ever.

Micro minds laugh hard, fooling insecurities found deep in themselves.
Kneeling is mental, lowering, lowering game, not your IQ though.
Walls are like bubbles, surfaces that keep borders. Are you in or out?
Blinders are self-built. A safety mechanism? For some, there's no choice.
Lives are crumbs to some. Swept away by cruel meanness. God really sees/cares?
Moments to enjoy can sneak into your mind-space and leave you breathless.
Exceptions to rules, forces beyond our control, steer us clear of sin.
Memories which last, need time to settle inward, contemplate their cure.
Sidewalks reflect souls, grinding or lightly stepping, depending on thoughts weight.
Consider relief, Release those worries that haunt. You can resolve this!
Accept no pressure. You are no prisoner of fear. Continue to beam.
Planning does not help. Life sways us every which way. Till you stop and think!
Portion your loving. Too extreme and you'll drown deep. Flotation device?
You are a treasure. Amaze yourself sometimes, please. Wonder at yourself.

Try Sleeping In An Antique Chair

Having fallen asleep in this large antique chair, the housekeeper forgot about her.

Busying herself with groceries, cleaning, phones, faxes, and gossip, the housekeeper forgot to check back on his visiting friend to tell her that he would be returning later than expected.

Her elbow was eventually seen, poking out from one side. When he rushed in, the evenings rays were cradled just above her head giving a halo effect to a mussed headed, makeup-streaked angelic face. He stared at her for few moments. He crouched beside her and listened to her (what must be a signature and almost imperceptible) snore. She sensed him there and awoke un-startled.

He leaned toward her, his apology in his face, and much more in his eyes. And while she is half-rested upon the arm of the armchair, they kissed each other for the first time.

When she said she was sorry she fell asleep, and it must be late and she should go, he asked if she had eaten and when she said no, but it's okay he told her not to move, to stay exactly still. They would eat something together since he hadn't eaten either.

The housekeeper was so apologetic and wringing her hands would have knitted a sweater right there if asked!
He only asked for salad, wine, figs, pears, and espresso.
The housekeeper ran inside for the food.
She was quicker than they anticipated, (or he's slow), because the lip lock almost took place when she reappeared. Now she is apologetically embarrassed and smiling while spilling the salads all over the table.

They all laugh.
Now she promises to leave them alone.
Of course, they'll put up the dishes and leftovers when done, so she was allowed to leave for the night. And grinning from ear to ear she is now wringing her hands for some other reason. And the skip in her step and twinkle in her eye, the eyebrow raising is very embarrassing.

She asked about his day. She can barely eat; they've become shy at looking at each other across the table. They laugh a lot, and finally relax, and they both think about the next one. You know.

He comes back to the chair. She straightens herself up-right now or (this time).

I Don't Weigh Much

As I sit here I watch my Mommy and Daddy; they both look so sad. Can't they see me waving and calling them? Why can't they hear me?

Dad: "I didn't mean to... it was an accident."

Mom: "Stop, it's my fault. I was bored. I wanted to make him jealous. My foolishness cost me my child, I caused this accident. Why would I need new underwear? I started wearing lipstick AND earrings around the house. I bought myself perfume, and vaguely explained the flowers I bought. She stood between us. When he was moving her aside, she slid on the just mopped floor. We heard a thud. Falling on his knees her Dad crawled over to her. She was limp. Cradling her…HE CRIED. Time meant nothing. I sat down near my baby and we rocked her. The police helped me to a chair. "

"They sound fuzzy now, it's hard to hear them.

Mom: "I was just trying to make him jealous by wearing earrings around the house and buying fancy underwear."

There's lots of people here! They fidget like I do here on this hard desk. I can almost reach the hammer, pens, and folders. This lamp I'm sitting near looks old, and these paper clips are big.

Mom:" She grazed the fridge." How long did I take? I don't know time anymore. I did this. It was an accident. Look at what we loss."

I feel wind against my face. I feel like I could fly. My Mommy always says that I don't weight much.

I always liked to swing at the playground, I liked to swing my legs and run. I can feel the wind against my face now. Maybe

Mommy and Daddy could take me to the playground when we leave here?

I am looking at Mommy and Daddy. They keep looking down. I guess they can't hear me. I am looking at a lot of other people. They can't sit still either. "Fidgeting", Mommy calls it.

Sitting on this hard desk, reminds me of the park. Park benches leave marks on your legs when you sit too long, and in the summer, my legs would stick.

Mom: "I was just trying to make him jealous by wearing earrings around the house and buying fancy underwear. I let him think there was someone else. Hell! I BOUGHT MYSELF THE FLOWERS! She stood between us. We froze when we heard the thud, then an eggshell cracking snap. She stood between us, he didn't mean it."

Dad: "I didn't mean it; it was an accident."

Mom: "He didn't mean it." He shoved her, she slid on the floor. We heard a thud when her head hit the floor. He dropped to his knees and crawled over to her. She shook for a few seconds then stopped. I grabbed my child, I screamed! I reached for the phone."

I usually wear ribbons, they swing by my ears, but I can't feel them now. I wish Mommy and Daddy would look up. This is some messy desk! Mommy wouldn't let me keep a desk like this! Paper clips, pens and papers everywhere. I made a necklace of paper clips once. I'll just sit here on my knees playing with these paper clips. I can almost touch this big stick that looks like a hammer Mommy uses on tough meat.

My Mommy told me that new babies are weighed on a scale. I wave to Mommy and Daddy. The lines in my hands are disappearing.

I called to them but there are so many people here, I guess they can't hear me.

There's lots of people here. They can't sit still. Mommy calls it fidgeting. I am fidgeting now because Mommy and Daddy won't look up and see me waving at them. I'll sit.

My butt is getting numb from sitting on this hard desk. My feet dandle over the edge. I'm not afraid because my hands hold either side near my knees, and I can swing my legs side to side.

I hear Daddy say "I didn't mean it."

I hear Mommy say "It's my fault."

I finish my paper-clip necklace. I swing it around my neck like a hula-hoop.

I stand and skip to Daddy. The necklace gets caught in the lamp. I swing off the edge, but nothing happens. Mommy says I don't weight much. The clip ends don't scratch me… today.

Oh look, crayons! I can draw. There's lots of paper here. Oh, oh… there's Auntie and Uncle. Auntie looks mad. Uncle looks glad. I don't want to see them. I would rather play with my crayons. I am too little to fight him. I showed Uncle my fist once, and he slapped me. He laughed at me. He said "What are you doing with that little fist? "You don't weigh much."

So, I'll go where it's safe. The library is nice and quiet; I wish I could stay with the books. There are lots of books next to me on this desk. They look heavy. I like stories. Neighbor lady reads to all of us kids. She reads about other countries and kids. She said she always liked to read from when she was a kid. I like pictures of faraway places too. I could live THERE, I could have good dreams. I took myself THERE to eat. I like to read too. I can tell time, but I forgot to look at the clock one day at neighbor lady's house. I came home again too late for supper, so I pretended I ate in my head. I told my belly to FEEEL FUULLL. The dinner I missed smelled SOOOO good.

Lying down here isn't so bad. I pretend it's not hard and cold here. I pretend I have a blanket. I rolled off once here, like I did off my bed. I tried to keep still. When I'm asleep I don't know that I move AN INCH, but if you said I did and I didn't remember then I rolled off the bed, hit something, and probably fell on a toy I LEFT out. I could roll off this, but only in my sleep, I'd be too scared awake!

Let me sleep, if I roll off, it's okay, I'll TRY NOT TO HURT ANYTHING, I haven't eaten, so I don't weigh much.

I didn't break the bed, although I was blamed again. How could I? I told neighbor lady I rolled off the bed like you said. That's not a bump neighbor lady…it's going away.

My mouth feels flat. Wet dribble is traveling down my chin, but I keep smiling. When I bounce up and down, my butt feels swishy and soft, and soggy. I want to play, but I can't sit up. My toes look fat; my fingers too. A breeze hits my head, I tumble, but it's okay cause I don't weigh….

A shoe on my leg, I am SORRY I cry. Jerked up to the sky, I fall, I see big feet, I am in the way. I'd move if I could, you're stepping on me, you're walking on me, but it's okay because, you know…

I'm in a bubble now. I feel wobbly. I can't see too clear. I hear sounds a little, then (water?) something pressing against me and I feel the (I smell the sea) sea, maybe I am dreaming,

I'll sleep, I FEEL FULL, I …. hmmm.

I worked with abused children in various settings which included court ordered residence, psychiatric clinic/hospitals, and as incarcerated adolescents.

Did I Become Extinct by Mother Nature

Did I become extinct
Because my eyes
Reminded you of the
,?

Nesting Straw

I have become like a nesting straw.
Windblown, sought for as a building block, weakened at times though still functional,
useful and rehabilitated for each avenue has climates.
I am malleable enough to provide comfort.
I have become more than nesting straw for others now realizing the strength of fibers and strands, the strength imbued by faith and promise by an ability to withstand
disappointment, disappearance, and choices that are not viable otherwise, so not real choices.
I have become a building material sagging and soaked, resilient yet fragile, steady and ready, reliable and let's not forget pliable.
I have become nesting straw fading, frayed, contorted and exhausted. Still strong in some areas, weakened in others, useless to some, useful to many, brave and resourceful, less blending in belief of others, unfolding, refolding, collapsing.
Nesting straw, not necessary yet necessary with temporary usefulness whether torn or discarded, repurposed by others, no one knows how many times pieces are freely used, baited and finally prohibited since it's the intentional fate of some nesting straw.
I will bind and almost blend elsewhere because I am nesting straw.
I am malleable enough to provide comfort.
Soothing replenishes each fiber, each strand ready for the next nest. Now each attempt wisely saving for eventual self-comfort someplace, somewhere, sometime; for I am nesting straw and I grow in knowledge cemented by each structure I build.
June 2023/ For Singapore Poetry Festival

Uses of Humor

Covering the uncomfortable
Harboring the harrowing
Making small of the
    Multitudinous wrongs
Uses of humor abound
Satirical
Self-aggrandizing
Insensitive
Lacking a punchline
Unless your audience
Fit the bill whether
They realize it or not
        Uses of humor
            Depend upon who's
        the butt of the joke.
Uses of humor depends upon the
    Sender's purpose, motive
Sense of superiority
Insecurity
Uses of humor can be caustic
Cause of trauma cause
Pain and the uses of
Humor can also provide
Relief, reprieve from
Pain and sorrow.
Laughter some call
    medicine
Laughter that doesn't
    Harm or lessen
    Others <u>is</u> medicine
Anything else is poison.
A poet's prompt from Between the Lines

Healing Unbound

Identify pain. Striking at cause is your fear. End it forever?
AWAKEN THE SELF! Seek help when you need it most.
CONFOUND NEGATORS!
Be kind to yourself. Pace your progress if needed. Enjoy living now!
Call, write, visit us. Keep journaling and talking. Make your sound clear. Take the aid freely. Address your causes of woe.
Leave gangsters behind.
Dismiss the sorrow. Fan away the flames of hate. Lovely one, be free.
Regain cartilage. Repair your spirit guiders. Revel in freedom.
Kiss your wounded soul. Your soul seeks your caressing. Quietly approach.
Understanding self. Quiet all storming clouding. Set your own pacing.
Relish learning YOU! The "Us" want to embrace you. Hope threads your wounds now.
Sigh away time lost. Emotions engine driven. Propel good mood swing.
Heal thyself prophets. Learn the help of others. Thoughts live, thrive on health.
Nurture your body. Care your spirits usefulness. Share this good knowledge.
Screen the naysayers. Clear your path of debris folks. With each tear, bud, leaf.
Nutrient rich love. Forgive yourself first, then them. Brightly shine with FRIENDS.
Healing takes time. PAUSE. Healing with positives helps.
Address, discard, THRIVE!
Debris on two feet. Appears human, has faults too! Please don't accept theirs.

Build safety triggers. Counter debris thrillers. They pray, eat and speak.
Sway, breathe, cry, write BLOOM! Learn the help of others. Share this good knowledge.

Red

I really don't feel like taking this darn basket through the woods! It's cold, the wind is cutting through my red bomber jacket and these open-toe sandals were a mistake. What was I thinking? What the heck is in this basket anyway?

Who's puts this much caviar, two jars of pearl onions, a wheel of cheese, crackers, anchovies, a bottle of merlot, a jar of dill pickle spears, and a tin of mixed nuts in one basket? What do I look like? A weightlifter? Delivering this is gonna take me for-evv-ver!

I heard rumors. This is why I deal with those wolves in town, especially the tall tooth-ful one always grinning when I pass by. I overheard him tell his pack, "She's got some Grandma! Wow! That calendar she did high-lighting her different moods each month was something else! He told them "I'm still in November!"

Why did I hook Grandma up to Zoom?

Salad Bar

The prongs of my fork shined bright with vinaigrette and
momentarily hovered above my thoughtfully arrayed bowl of
greens. Upon deciding to commence with luscious fronds
suddenly
a vein in a leafy green opened and became a mouth.
And I was speechless.
The vein in the leaf that opened and became a mouth developed
lips and shouted obscenities
and I was speechless.
The vein in the leaf that became a mouth developed lips then
snarled and barked at me
and I was speechless.
The vein in the leaf twisted and turned yellow, reddish-brown
then green and yellow again
and I was speechless.
The vein in the leaf that became a mouth barred its teeth, pointy
and sharp
And I was speechless.
The vein in the leaf that became a mouth, apologized, and
pleaded for help
And I was speechless.
The vein in the leaf that became a mouth grinned at me, like
a dare
And I was speechless.
Yes, I was speechless.
The vein in the leaf that became a mouth with lips developed a
tongue and tried to kiss me
And I was speechless.
The vein in the leaf that became a mouth with lips and a tongue,
I ate in one gulp
And the leaf was speechless, or so I thought at first.

The leaf grumbled part way down my esophagus then tried to use my voice box so you could hear.

This leaf opened my mind. I heard sobbing in my head.
The vein in the leaf that became a mouth, shared my mouth by baring my teeth, forcing my grin and gave this message" You created me and now I'll consume you."
I heard the grinding of teeth then realized it was my own.
The vein the leaf that became my mouth had a litany of speeches all complaints about mealy soil, overly aggressive bugs, questionable water, and artificial lighting and indelicate harvesting.
I turned yellow, green, reddish- brown and yellow again. I pointed to the salad bar, and the greens turned yellow, reddish-brown, then green again.
In the process kale gave me the middle finger, parsley smirked, chicory winked, and the curly romaine tried to mumble a joke.
My gastric juices told off the leaf I swallowed that developed a mouth, lips, teeth and tongue from it's vein.
My body became quiet again once the leaf was expelled, flushed, and drowned away. Morale: Eat your damn greens; just reconsider the salad bar.
Fun Fiction

Mirror, Mirror, On The Bus Back Door, Who's the Fareless of Them All?

Well, who's the fairest in the land?

If ever in doubt watch riders traveling from north to south on an express bus.

"Who's the Fareless In the Land? Mass Transit Fare Operates best if you're blonde, over fifty-five and the fairest in the land, because favors them now. Board members, wives, sisters perhaps too some need two seats, one for them and perhaps their new packaged tutus.

White, Black, Brown, Yellow and Tan, people pay their fares, and a few shades of various hues pay their card dues . On the carousel of city transit to their destinations, they put their cards ready in handheld expectation. Somehow the fares of the fairs get lost, but one has to register that rides cost money and have expirations. Well, heh, heh, not really if you leave home with only charge card money.

No one arrests children of the 'fair just screen for tanned, get nabbed or flattened. The fairest in the land would never be asked, much less accosted, no officer would dare address their theft via awkwardness, But for me. need a quota filled? which on me would be a grievous act, completing a ticket, embarrassment and maybe cuff, while the fairness of the less, would hardly be muffed

Express busses especially. If you enter at upper avenues, sit down, watch the sidewalks, look around at the views. No wallet, no omni no fare graces their manicured tips because the rest of us are the ones stiffed.

Entering through the middle or back doors of the bus fair game for the fairest in the land. Look who's preferring the back of the bus now, middle at least, but not the very public view of up front seats, unless the wrinkles win sympathy and smile sweet.

I'm one of the most fared in the land because I pay for my rides, no sly. No limbo rocking or crawling under turnstiles no leaping over gates or slithering through emergency door plates

Watch the fareless in the land, love the side and backdown jams, because not paying and proud of too, no shame, in their game, got nothing to lose.

Jeeves must be off, and the vault is on a timer, no problem, time for nails, cocktails and fruit smoothie manna. It must be nice to travel for free, it appears so for certain the fareless in the land, don't look like me.

Non-Fiction

National Piss Off Day

International Slap Your Annoying Co-Worker Day, **always on October 23rd**, I missed decades of opportunities to enact this, and I'm ticked!!!

I looked up mismanagement and got **June 14th** is World Anti-Nepotism Day, again kept conveniently secret. This day was instituted to honor those who lost their lives due to depression and harassment because of nepotism in any field. Bollywood's Sushant's spirit can tell you why (S. Singh Rajput) he's in another realm.

International Anti-Corruption Day is **December 9th,** so who-knew, the corrupt kept us in the dark intentionally, It's also missing from company issued calendars. We know why!!!

July 7th is Global Forgiveness Day, good luck with that, I'm a pessimist just keeping it real and trying to limit negativity. Did you notice?

Now I'm on a mission to make up for those lost dates, thank God these dates get repeated each year! I'll pattern-code and cross-reference them for easy future reminding. Glory, glory. I can add a few "with flavor".

National Hot Sauce Day is January 22nd Still time to honor at least a few international days. National Hot Chocolate Day was January 31st, No problem. I put cayenne in my hot chocolate anyway Boo- yah! Blew that up didn't I.

Fin Hall's "National Piss Off Day" Prompt. Here's my response June /2022.

Mr. Hall hosts a monthly open mic from Scotland titled "like a bolt from the blue."

I Collect Ice Cream Coupons

Ice cream cools palates and sometimes moods, but not always. We always ate our ice cream in silence because flavor doesn't offset tantrums unless the tongue is permanently dulled.
Drugged ice cream was on Dana's menu more than once, and worked like a charm each time. Large scoops Dana served up on waffle cones and pies, in shakes and sundaes, of course recipients were unaware that it's their last meal.
Dana tired of boastful people. Dana tired of foul-language, tired of bullies, tired of those who belittle others by their conversation. Dana hardly spoke but felt knowing them this way and sizing them up was enough. Their body language, overpowering physicality, and gruff tone got some new flavor taste-tasting scoops. Yum. Not. Taste buds be damned.
Dana's elders shouldn't have slapped Dana's plate of ice cream on the floor and command Dana lick it up.Children remember. Dana apparently neither forgot nor forgave. Dana grew up and gave back.
Dana 's insistence of a pre-meal toast for their family reunion dinner was actually the beginning of their undoing. The coroner said Dana provided a wonderful five-course dinner, serving ice cream for dessert.
When cutting food and forking one's ear instead of mouth, apparently more than depth perception is a problem. No? Along with appreciable sloppiness and horrible table manners, their stunning revelation of eminent immobility was palpably sarcastic; given the bindings inflicted upon Dana's childhood both mentally and physically. Now, they felt tight leather bondage. Now, surrounded my mirrors they experienced eye-widening fear. Pictures of waterfalls pinned on the drawn drapes barely satisfies their quicksand repeating thirst that cheek saliva could not quench. Why? Dana discovered the family's heritage was a

morbid propensity for cheating death. Controlling death is also addictive.

True, Dana admitted it looked difficult for them to swallow their force-fed ice cream with the dog collar around their necks, but after all it was the only food they would ever taste again, in this lifetime.

Groveling… let me tell you, it's not pretty. Its debasing, pathetic, Dana had to take a shower after watching their bodies twitching and begging.

Come on, doesn't a hot bath or shower reinvigorate you too? I'm just a reporter. No, I lied. I'm a Dana groupie. I digress, back to Dana.

Dana loves opera. Those high notes and woeful low notes really capture the awe and shock when folks ABSORB their fate. You mean this is how I'm going to die? their faces said. Huh, huh. Dana responded.

Dana's testimony was riveting. No reason to lie, Dana gave them their just desserts. That's what Dana's family always said when Dana was forced to stay with them. "Your parents were trash," Dana's elders would shout. "You'll never find them, they're good as dead," which was always followed by their communal "wink, wink." Now we're stuck with you!"

Why was I born Dana would often wonder? I didn't ask to be born! Dana told the jury that "Practice makes perfect" so yes this "Last Supper" required testing on customers and was pre-meditated. At least I know where and how I'm going to die Dana said. Dana's last meal? Ice cream and Pagliacci . Dana has been sentenced. Dana will never be out. I thank Dana or my new profession. My occupational nice, so to speak.

I'm selling ice -cream now, and looking for an outlet. Would you like to invest? I can bring you in on the ground floor. Friends and family day specials coming soon.

Fiction

I Can't Believe I Got Dressed Up For This!

What a sham! The write up and "exotic-ti-que" cocktails promised, the fuu-fuu food selections and multi-ethnic, fusion inspired cuisine- Ha!

Wore my gold and good shoes! What!

In fact, the photos online in reality show the only two festive looking, high quality impressively furnished walls in the entire place.

On top of that, get this; some folks looked like they just came back from shopping at Target. Sit down!

Ordered a drink. It was fancily flamed at my table – it sucked! I can't believe I got dressed up for this!

Non-Fiction

Halloween

He didn't visit often, barely spoke to us, but occasionally when visiting he'd bring a pie.

He worked at a bakery franchise and came with a pie. How nice.

I opened the pie after he left, and dinner was over. As I cut into the pie, it started oozing a blood like color. I never saw a pie do that before. I proceeded with the surgical skill of a seven-and-a-half-year-old now trusted and deemed responsible enough to cut with a REAL adult butter knife. I cut a second mark, and upon attempting to lift the triangular slice out with our pie spatula, I saw it.

An off-white, long, slender, roughly edged "bone." I jumped back from the table. I gasped. I put the butter knife down. The pie was still bleeding. It was seeping out onto the crust. I was immobilized. I found a bone in a pie.

Even chicken pot pie doesn't have bones and only bleeds peas, carrots, celery pieces, potatoes, and brown gravy. I've had cherry pie, and I was very well acquainted with apple pie, blueberry pie too. I knew coconut and pumpkin pies; even made pineapple upside down cake. I saw pictures of Boston cream pie and lemon meringue pie; NONE BLEED.

I was a child that enjoyed reading encyclopedias. One had the human anatomy shown on peel away transparent sheets that showed veins, then bones, then muscles, then flesh, all as overlays that when assembled with our dermal layers shows the body as we see it. There's a lot working under our skin!

Someone's missing a piece.

It's still oozing. Pie crust is a poor bandage but a good sponge, now a flaky deep red bloody looking crust.

I ventured a look at the side of the box for a label. Huh, never saw that word before, but I'm not up to the "R's" yet.

I went to the trusty encyclopedia and looked it up. I read the first paragraph. It's a real food grown in America. I went back to the table. I'll be all right. I lifted out the cut piece with our pie spatula. The piece of crust had green strings sauced with goo attached which I placed into my mouth. I felt like a brave pioneer. I closed my mouth. It made my lip pucker and burn citrusy-like, like when if you bit your lip skin away and ate a sour orange right afterwards. This is tart and bitter, I think. It wasn't even sweet! Dessert pies are supposed to be sweet! Isn't there a law that they have to have a certain amount of sugar content to be labeled dessert pie? The green strings were trying to choke me. I left the bone stalks in the plate which still looked like a femur. These vein-like things were trying to choke my (newly discovered fun word) EP-Pi-Glot-Tis. I felt warm and sinking fast, I could see the dramatic headlines "Little Girl Killed By Bloody Celery Pie." I hear myself gurgling. I spit it out. In my head I'm thinking "Don't waste food; children in Africa are starving." I tried. I wouldn't even wish this on them, even though THEY ARE STARVING! If I had an allowance, I'd send them the money instead of the scary bloody celery pie!

I return to my trusty encyclopedia. To my surprise, we hold festivals make relishes, muffins, and candy with this? Yes! Annual rhubarb festivals are held May through October in several parts of the world where this cool temperature vegetable, with POISIONOUS leaves is grown. Scare - reee.

Non-Fiction

I Shot Thought into the Air

I shot Thought into the air, and it fell back down around me.
"I have no wings, I'm not fully developed!" Thought decried claiming prematurity.
I said "Oh you'll be fine, trust instinct, would you please! Don't deny what you have to bring to the world community."
Thought replied: "But I'm not ready. I was wrong begging to be freed."
"Consult the stars." I said to Thought. "I trust you'll return back safely, and if not it's because you have a calling beyond my level or capacity."
Thought replied: "But you set me up and about the air, you just released me, I saw you!"
Maybe YOU HAVE THE RIGHT TO BE ALIVE and who believes you, well it's their choice.
Sounding strong and reassuring reminding Thought of my privileged role I continued: "I am a vessel holding many ideas warming them until just the right time. I try to melt away ideas, fears and doubts which may or may not be benign. You see the possibility of being misconstrued is because as your progenitor and muse, the blame will rest solely on me as the one who birthed such as you. You see, I must have faith in you Thought although you could be abused. I am sure within my heart dear Thought we grow bolder with each view. So kindly dear one so close to me, believe in you as I do and we will both be redeemed. You might find like-minded friends who know what has substance versus clownish demeaning, or die trying to be fertile and new."
Thought pondered and seemed less dazed and confused, a bit of the trepidation soon dismissed from view.
"I guess you're right," Thought offered as an olive branch and salve, expecting wounding will come since we think alike, as complimenting halves.

"We are worth the work dear Thought," I measured. "Change only comes when brave and challenge is not demurred. We are good, kind, and peaceful, not stupid, not cowardly not tamed. The good you could do dear Thought is worth whatever disdain. The battle has been coming to us, while we gently held our ground, the quicksand is frothing over there as swallowing abounds."

"Yes you're right of course," Thought replied. "I was made not to rest but to amplify."

Thought underscored such thinking then puffed-up tripling in size.

"A sound bite without substance is worthless," I replied. "An annoying buzz in someone's ear isn't worth a reply. Make your message sound and clear and inclusive to those who do more than hear. Make sure you can stand alone because detractors come in all shapes and sizes, huge smiles and all kinds of wiles, cunning and derisive.

Your humility powers your energy, you are ignited by constructive synergy, no one takes advantage of you unless they have no heart.

Many also have an empty cavity when brain and spinal cord meet, they only operate in conjunction when fleeing with both feet. But I use that brain cavity as your cradle, rocker, and your highchair for years. I'd love you, Thought, whether actualized in this time warp or not," I said as I fought back my tears.

"I will continue beckoning you," Thought energetically praised. "And every once in awhile I'll come back for strengthening and your gaze. I know you're always with me progenitor and muse, our lifelines are entangled there is no better place I'd tether and refuel."

The prompt was "Right versus Privilege" provided by the Nuyorican Café.

Bare Tyres (Tires)

I am tired
like a worn- out tire.
My grooves have been
worn down and
so, I am tired.
Like wheels
of rubber on a
Vehicle, I am
ridden till bare,
through storms, sand
and grasses.
I have treads like
My braids that bespeak
my birthplace, my
heritage, factory
specific and stamped.
I am tired like a
worn out tire.
But I still roll,
roll on with worn
threads, and still move.
A poet's prompt

Sides

I spout when consumed with raw emotion, so charged not on horseback, but in your fields.
So charged my energy spouts tears and the tearing of families so familiar to some while business as usual for others.
An energy you feel, you see. You witness, believe in, so you promote, cause repeatedly unashamed, unabashedly and proudly advertise bearing and profited sweltering wealth.
An energy with strength, still not fully unleashed, released like evaporating sweat on many bent brows tethered to this foreign soil with debilitating work so I bleed trying to untether from this soil. I till. I toil. I am the soil, for I watered it before your spouting.
The spouting of voluminous tears, misting all over slavery fogging the flogging Bible spoken, pew carving "Good ole Boys!"

You spoke up? In the twilight, not the dawn, not the daytime, just the evening of your years. Spouting gently so as not to frighten: just enough misting one awake and make aware?
Gently I leave openings for insight, each layer offers an embroidery of light.
Sourcing air for one to breathe, flow and mix with air both beneath and above.
Same as our thoughts, our dialogue mixes like air.
Above, around and below and without sound, a feel, a touch, stances that watch me as I encourage your mind to dream around the concept of equal peace.
You want to touch me. You want to stroke these meandering thoughts and hope to cajole voices to agree.
Stagnation is already fraught with contamination! I listen to history; it's why I was born. Bending light, lessening shade, and lifting; opposites of what you once believed?

Via air, the rustling of documents changing the tide, changing the victory war cry, changing the accent on "whooping-it-up," gasping from alternate lips and throats genteel once a lilac-lemon perfumed accented "Oh my heavens!" became back shack sun lashed sweat perfumed accented "Lawdy-be!"
Call on a win, victory your prayers, hopes for freedom between each lattice swear. Voices between land and cripped overworked gnarled hands. Shake on it?
Bands of lights flames and sheet hiders between my lattice cower in historical nightmare plain sight. Forcing ever upward and heard on each droplet, transparent winged clouds forcing families asunder.
Ever upward waiting for a solution filled response. Still waiting for both sides to agree at the apex point physics cannot ever attain without our equally representative non-alloy lessening bending.
I do not stand dormant; I am alive with every sentence memorized.
I know your speeches, your intent, I find space within my lattice, always room for anyone finding, seeking, promoting some workable non-exclusionary and genuine, unbiased sense!
Above, around and below and without sound, a feel, a touch, stances that watch me as I encourage your mind to dream around the concept of equal peace.
Not named in the legacy you thought, for fate and faith you do not command, no orders do you spout except from the malevolent mealy mouthed.
Listened for a cause they want to resurrect, listen for the call we civilly want to lay rest and won't until there is full digest, confess, and never a regress.
Claim to wicked fame, blood kin generation once removed except this curving of light will be removed, still remembered, curved and fashioned expertly with deft script and command with twice imbued artistry.
There is a time, never forgotten, forever engraved on tombstones

and hearts carved within the shadows of minds, oral histories
and printed and monumented too.
Curved, scalloped light, multiplied shaded might, such historical
slights provide much needed insight.
Ekphrastic response to Longfellow Fountain, USC courtyard, built twice by Allan J. Sindler. Permission by his son Michael Sindler, poet and artist.

Our Flag

I wave the flag of the United States of America not the flag of surrender solid white as some would prefer because your preference doesn't make this land. America's landscape is diverse just as those who inhabit her by intent, slave trade and indigenous birth.

Yes, I wave the flag of the U.S. of America not the flag of surrender solid white as some would prefer. I wave "Hi. Hello." not good-bye exposing my pink palm topped with black, brown tan, yellow, red, and navy-blue, red-veined, and friendship-pored skin.

I wave the flag of the United States of America, not the flag of surrender, solid white as some would prefer. I wave my black arms tanned forever from birth across America, seen in daylight, lunchtime and ebony bright in your headlights. I wave the flag of us that makes some cringe, who spit on this shared ground when I tread upon it which of itself is both criminal and absurd.

I wave the flag of the United States of America not the flag white (no surprise) you prefer for I am American whether you like it or not. I am not demurred for I will not be decimated as you tried through sport to kill native buffalo herds.

Yes, I wave the flag of the U.S. of America, a land never lost so not founded by a few. A land already alive and living vibrant, pristine, and treasured in-spite of some denying those and them automatically and naturally born free while remembering the red -skinned indigenous fooled into trusting the white, those who introduced their white flag from their losing combats. Blue boo-hued to the sky were cries to white clouds and stars, these witnesses to criminal, cultural ignorant racists profiteers sourcing tribes' demise.

Yes, I wave the flag of the "US" of America, not the flag of surrender, colored pure white as some would prefer. I wave my head high in white clouds laden full of tears that watered this landscape when white men appeared. Beige-ed clouding floating in a blue sky when red men families rode in fear. I wave my hands clasped and cringed in desperation because some do not want me heard. Freely I can fight wars and conflicts for those who think America only belongs to them. How is it that I can return, bruised, beaten and homeless in the same US land?

Because I wave the flag of the US of America for veterans' brave and scolded "Damn, you returned, survived and still humming?" I do not think some feel much concerned or beholden. Some others wave the flag of the US of America cling to this faith red, white and, blued the "white dinged" which look at me incredulously say this flag is not attributed to those and them and you.

I wave the flag of the U.S. of America not the flag of surrender, white as some would prefer. I wave my voice within octaves of pain, cries, angered shouts. marrow deep, eyelash vibrating shrill not succumbing to verbal, psychological, social, and physical abuse. I am not here for your sport.

I wave the flag of the US of America, not solid white as some would prefer Despite what some others may prefer, we share the flag, and you do not get to choose who hold, waves and kneels and pledges to this inclusive flag that makes some cringe and divert their eyes for I am American despite what some may assert, and I will not be denied for while you shout back at me "Drop dead! Leave already! Go back, we wish to remain pure white! I have not that intention as some would prefer. I wave the same flag from my Porsche or porch despite what flag you think appropriate for me.

I wave the flag of the "US" of America, not the flag of surrender, colored pure white as some would prefer. This landscape bold and free is also mine, not requiring your approval. My proof is my word proven by reams of legal, vetted, honored, respected politically earned. voted, debated, warranted, indemnified American sanctioned Congressional. Senate, Constitutional and protected truths against some holding dear temporary useless biased beliefs, gangster money, and desperately disingenuous power lust.

Finally, understand, I wave the flag of the United States of America, not solid white as some would prefer, because I will not surrender what this country, my country, our country which my people and others of color continue to fix, amend, and preserve the best of this human herd. By my combined spiritual and undeniable right, I'll not wave away my birthright as some of you would concur.

Non-Fiction

This Orb

This orb- glistening blue and
Green protected
By air columns
Artificially transfixed
For us.
This orb- gliding upon the
Web of space like
A toy in the hands
That made her
This orb - slowly we strangle,
we suffocate by
our waste, greed
amorous disregard
and sloth
This orb- Surviving on life support because of us the virus that
she required we wear KN95's to protect us from the virus she
made to get us to work together and almost failed to do. The
lesson this orb tried to teach us to live as shared species across,
around, within her ...
but I digress,
This orb- we need to soothe
Back to health
Give her our respirators
She needs to wear a KN95 from us the
Virus that kills her
This orb – is the patient
we infect
with our noise and fights
and threats!
This orb – is where I live
With you and her resuscitation
Requires team

Work – I can't
Breathe
echoes from
street death to sky
This colored orb cries the same
"I can't breathe."
So, by default, we don't either.

Passioned Learning

Learning requires minds lined with poetic pieces ringed with
highly winged singers, likened sirens.
Listen. Whisper their melodies.
Swing. Swing again. Swing, sigh, smile again. Learning again.
Timelessly, again.
Blindly wild passioned learning is fruitful, searingly mindful,
lasting, beautiful, gloriously lined with wisdom.
Growing is gained via steaming winds, learning requires minds
lined with poetic pieces ringed with highly winged singers,
again whispered, swing, sigh, blindly wild learning, propelling
minds, again, timelessly, again.
Shaping requires minds lined with poetic pieces,wild images
propelling learning, encouraging minds, likened sirens, melodies
timelessly again, wind winds again, whisper again, hearing,
repeating.
Listen. Learning timelessly.
Forming requires life, requires attention.
Respite? Which wording is misunderstood? Their melodies live!
Listen. Learning timelessly.

Katalyst Colvin developed/coined this poetic form Cyclops Poetry since each word contains only one letter "I." She co-hosts "Open Minds" an open mic venue conducted from Canada with her husband Thomas Colvin. Here I am inspired to share another poet's format thus promoting our shared creative progress by utilizing this form.

Mother Nature Tempers... Flowing

Mother Nature tempers momentarily her hot anger at the invaders trampling her native sons and daughters. They understand her waves of heat and flowing red fingertips, brightening the whips, the lines across their backs, their legs of so many natives everywhere multiplied.

We survived all that and more, the taunts, the misuse, the intentional misguidance. Rewarded with ...

I Have Only Two Minutes With You Tonight

I have only two minutes with you tonight so consider why this pandemic occurs, and cause.
Consider our response positively.
Consider, consider again and decide your role as an individual and
then with my remaining minute
I suggest we consider each other and those we hold dear.
And wish to yet discover as cause to positively change or add to our combined expiration.
Consider our limited time.
Consider our responsibility to each other.
Consider the potential for good. I do believe we each have good potential in some way, deeper inward in some rather than in others.
My time is soon up. Yours will follow. I tried my best.
Can you say the same? I am still considering what is "the best".
My time is up, so is yours. Use time wisely. I am trying. Maybe we can add our two minutes together and reach an infinity?
Fiction: Nuyorican Café prompt as the title states.

Part Four

THE PLAY

"E & O"

Prologue

Life beholds promise/I am happily bursting!/I smile like a fool/ Everyone sees us and laughs!/Wishing they were us no doubt!

Going onward dear /I willingly surrender/Soft fields like tresses/ bird's songs mimic your lilt voice/ We harmonize night star lights

I -The Wedding

Welcoming Guests

VOICE OF E:

1-This is a brightness/I will keep you warm by me/Love has gifted me/Swirl to oppose gravity/Gaiety, levity sing!

2-This is a brightness/Gaiety, levity sing!/Today our pledging/Promises binding our love./I am tortured by waiting.

VOICE OF O:

3-You are an aura/You fill every thought I have./Love has gifted me/Your aura without perfume./Heavy breaths synchronize hearts.

4-Love has wrapped me up/ I love to unwrap these gifts./Unwrapping your heart /My desire fills me up./I sing to your, lit thighs.

5-Find gifts in swaddling/You break me down so gently/Find gifts un-yielding/Cool at first your soft lit thighs/Breathing on your soft lit thighs.

VOICE OF E:

6-Strum my lyre strings love/Cascading notes through nibbles/Heated to blister/Your kisses serve AS MY salve/Enjoying fervent healing.

VOICE OF O:

7-Gladly I find wounds/I oppose gravity too!/Unwrap a cool head/Rippling on your lit thighs/Blushing guests as intended.

8-Love has wrapped me up/I love to unwrap these gifts/Find gifts in swaddling/Cascading with each nibble/I love to unwrap these gifts.

9-Willful your binding/Cascading with each nibble/Unwrap your heart dear/Cascading with each nibble/Breathing on these lit thighs.

VOICE OF E:

10-Breaking me down gently/Singing to these soft lit thighs/Strum my lyre strings love/Blushing guests as intended/Gaiety, levity sing!

VOICE OF O:

11-Unfold such perfume/An aura will satisfy/Though palmed and heated/Skipping through those soft lit thighs/Such intoxicating limbs!

12-An aura my love/Skipping to the brightened light/Find gifts un-melting/Cascading with each nibble/An intoxicant each limb.

II- Gait Bait

Voice of O:

13-Your smile wakens birds/Who do you meet on your stroll?/Your gaiety shines/Your eyes color everyone./Kindly you rouse each being.

14-You walk everyday/Your form alluring to all/Sure soft stepped your gait /Who watches you as you stroll?/Everyone knows of your stroll.

15- OH, EVERYONE KNOWS/Kindly you rise each being/Your soft clean boned limbs/Who do you meet on your stroll?/Who amuses in your gait?

Voice of E:

16-Why their cruel intent?/My arms are bruised from tangling/Tripping upon what?/My foot is bruised from catching/Head swimming, bruised from catching.

17- I am preyed upon!/I fear for no bush hides me/Do not tender me!/I hum to one melody/Dazed I fall upon this ground.

18-Evil their intent./My arms are bruised from catching/Freedom, oh so brief!/Four lusted eyes upon me!/Head swimming bruised from catching.

19-Freedom, oh so brief!/My foot is bruised from catching/ See four lusted eyes/Short breaths now bruised from catching/Both smiles slithering away.

20-Two villains' laughter/ Two times I tried outrunning Two demons' laughter/Four lusted eyes witnessed death./ Smiling as they slither on.

21-I am preyed upon/My senses betray their loss./Dazed I fall on ground/I fear for no bush hides me./Four lusted eyes upon me.

22-These partners in crime/My arms are bruised from falling/Two foes stinging me/Four lusted eyes won this day/This is the cause as I swell.

23- My eyes are less dim/Bruising from catching I fear/Two villains' laughter/Two lusted eyes then upturned/Smiling as they slither on.

24- Tripped upon nothing?/Four lusted eyes ran my way/Twine, rope or something/Four lusted eyes watched me pray/Four lusted eyes witnessed death.

25- Partners in crime action./Four lusted eyes won this day/Root vine entangled/This bruising painful ache and swell/Demons' laughter known so well.

26-I was preyed upon!/Four lusted eyes watched me pray/ Too slowly fate won/Eyes dimming bruised from catching/Smiling as they slither on.

27- OH, EVERYONE KNOWS/Two times I tried outrunning/Evil their intent/Smiling as they slither on/Four lusted eyes won this day.

III-"Surrendering Aloud"

Voice of O:

28-Gift me such wounding!/Are your lashes long as well?/How sweet those ankles!/Was your grasp as tight as mine?/Please grasp my throat, kiss my lips.

29-Tooth an invader/I un-swaddle before you./Gift me such wounding./Take my breast, thigh, leg, each arm./Only kiss me too, please, please!

30-How sweet each pearled toe/Recalling smooth high arches/How sweet these ankles!/Sand, Dirt, Stone thorn invaders?/Such wounding I cannot bear!

31-An invaders tooth/I un-swaddle before you!/Gift me such wounding/Fear me not, I welcome you!/Grasp my throat, kiss my lips.

32-I would kiss each scale/Write love songs to your hissing/But I can't catch one/A note my lyre would feign praise/You prey upon massive loss.

33-Grasp at my dying/Fateful my agonizing/Pleasuring foul ones/They escape my grasp so well/Prey now upon my dear loss .

VOICE OF E:

34-I welcome nothing/Noon and night look the same now/ My senses are closed/I am numbed so don't mind me/Vows echo in stone chambers.

35- Emotions bind me/My heart like this cavern scolds/My heart feels no more,/Where is my light, my lover?/My heart like this cavern scolds.

36- My heart is stopping/Fear has no home without you/Anomaly, me?/My heart's loss echoes screaming/My thoughts are fogged with venom.

37- My heart was just mined/Fear has left me with nothing/My heart suffocates/Holding mold and weak sinews/Who doesn't mind anymore?

38- My heart strangles me/Stumbling is a strange comfort/Circumference of fear?/A path without escaping/No longer caring for self.

IV Wounding Tonic

Voice of O:

39-My heart deflates now/My heart like this cavern scolds/I had a heart once/My soul like this cavern dry./My spirit like caverns molds.

40-My sight useless now/Oh my method will find thee/I no longer weep/My resolve is unfailing/Fear has no home, no rest here.

41- Fear has no seat here/I am hounded by my thoughts/My resolve is pure/Fear has no home without you/My spirit like this cavern molds.

42 -Going onward dear/This darkness will bring me light./ You shine in these depths./You illuminate my steps/My method will find thee.

43- My knowing heart drums/Dull and hollow all music/Fear finds no repose/Now my mind drums one handed/I strum as a lonely soul.

44- Music tears me up!/ I no longer anything/I no longer weep/We fill a sack of loose bones/I am hounded by my thoughts.

45- A chase that chose you/My resolve is unfailing/Quick bite, fang delight/Your fear, your fall, your tumble/Two demons leapt at my dear.

46- I wasn't nearby/I am hounded by these thoughts/I needed to stay/Two demons leapt at my dear/A glint in their eyes for you.

47- I should have died, Why?/Because I wasn't nearby/Beneath me you walk/I am hounded by these thoughts/No, not your sky darkening.

48- Tree limbs see me bleed/ Trees refuse to hold my weight/I water like dew/Their branches catch tears and sobs/Trees refuse to hold my weight.

49- Do you hear my stomp?/This darkness will bring me light/You shine in these depths/You illuminate my steps/strengthened by my memories.

50- Echoing to you/Our wedding intoxicant!/Smell father's larkspur/Dear, please take my sad pleading soul/I willingly surrender.

V - Resolve

Voice of O :

51- Does the sun still shine?/Do you hear my mind storming?/I no longer wish to cry/Do you hear my mind storming?/I want to harvest your arms.

VOICE OF E :

52-I water like dew/Love, I am no longer dulled/Does the sun still shine?/I curse this eternity/No Gaiety? Levity?

VOICE OF O:

53-Sorrowing alone/Hunger is told to vanish/ My thirst is tear quenched/I no longer sigh wishes/Every blade mimics your hair.

54- You live within me/I long for my lovely one/Lips as elixir/Love be not a memory/I curse your eternity.

VOICE OF E:

55- You water my tomb/ Closing eyes facing skyward/ Roots now my tendrils/You are picking flowers there/I no longer weep, I sob.

56- You curse at my tomb/You scratch your name on my tomb./You lie on my tomb/You scratch your name on my tomb/The ground betrays your outline.

57- You soak my tomb/You are picking flowers there/Their roots betray you/Treading while screaming my tomb/Weeding my tomb with your knees.

58- You sleep on my tomb./Weep together my lover/You lie on my tomb/Burrowing till cramping hands/We share burrowing one tomb.

Voice of O:

59-Bees mimic your hum/They learned from you my lovely/The breeze trails your voice/Speak to me on spider webs/ Your tears suspended dew drops/One loving one taken love.

60-How clever my love!/Shared our cursed eternity/Never severing/I too pine away all time /Our common, soulless pain.

61-As creatures spin tales/Carefully each web is read/They are notes my dear/They crawl where you abide now/I follow so willingly.

62-I will dry my tears/ Crawling in both dark and day./You message me dear./I curse your eternity./Away from loves nesting place.

63-I failed you again!/I held our eternity/Sorrowful sighing!/I caused this eternity/I beg all vice obtain me.

64- Sorrow is depthless/This shadow has no life now/Sorrow loves shadows/Even the earth won't take me!/Look, every cave rejects me.

Voice of E & O:

65-When so close the sky/Closing eyes, facing skyward/When close to abide/A furnace bronzes below/Our common, soulless pain.

66-Stars patrol our tomb/Blushing guests as intended/ Skyward we abide/Cascading with each nibble/We harmonize night star lights

67- From loving just you/Blushing guests as intended./Inspiring lovers' dreams/My palm upraised behind me/Oh, where are your fingertips?

68- My fingertips fear/Oh, where are your fingertips?/My fingertips stretch/My paces are breathless now/My fingertips sense longing.

69- My fingertips arch/My paces are breathless now/Reach, arch, ache alone /Dying returns to us both /Limbs once you fondled limp now.

70- My feet leave no print/My feet are lead leaden thighs/ My feet lead my groin/Away from loves nesting place/One loving, one taken love

71- Roots now are tendrils/I hunger for my dear one./ Strings Dare not to sound./Notes rebound in hollowed sound/I am tortured by waiting.

<u>VOICE OF E:</u>

72-My sky remains wormed./Toes feeding thin long seedlings./With time I will branch./Will caress your napping brow/Beloved swing in my lap.

73- A furnace bronzes/Flames inhabit my sockets/Nothing left to view/Limbs once you fondled limp now/Who wishes they are us now?

WAKA attempt

Part Five

NONOGRAM

TBB NonOgram Directions

Nonograms are picture logic puzzles where cells on a grid must be either filled in or remain blank according to numbers appearing at the edges of the grid. These numbers represent continuous blocks of filled squares within that column or row.

If the column or row has multiple numbers, you must separate them by empty white squares.

Once completed a picture will be revealed

Solution Suggestion : If the row or column is the entire length or takes up most of the grid line, fill these columns or rows first.

						1	1	1		1	1	1			
				1	2	1	1	1	6	1	1	1	2	1	
			1						X						
			3					X	X	X					
	1	1	1				X		X		X				
	1	1	1			X			X			X			
	1	1	1		X				X				X		
			11	X	X	X	X	X	X	X	X	X	X	X	

TBB Nonogram

			3													
			3												5	
			1			12				2		7	3	1	3	5
			1	15	15	2	4	4	3	1	4	4	10	12	1	1
		13														
	11	2														
7	3	2														
6	3	3														
3	1	3														
	4	3														
	4	4														
	4	4														
	3	3														
	3	2														
	3	2														
	3	4														
	3	3														
	3	3														
	4	3														

(Answer key at the back of the book)

Part Six

DANGA

Skip ahead to Page 221

EXTRA
Meteor hoping is dangerous.
Where's the suds in soap operas?
I was once like Yous.
Hope to wake up soon!
PREVIEW
Note taking
Seriously, I need a new gig.
Clean up on aisle Andromeda
Is it me or do some centuries Seem longer than others?

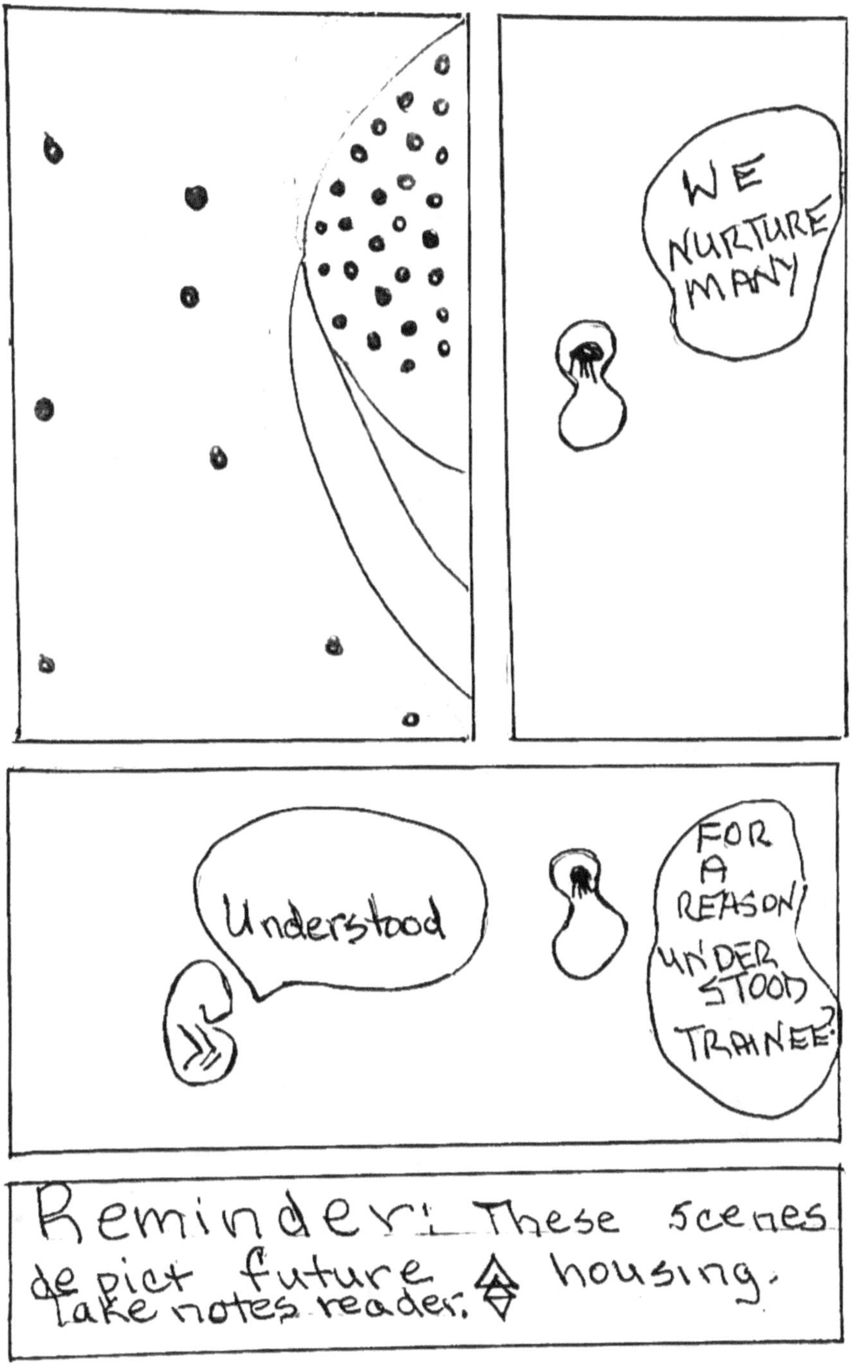
WE NURTURE MANY
Understood
FOR A REASON UNDERSTOOD TRAINEE?
Reminder: These scenes depict future housing. Take notes reader.

What galaxy are you from again?
Being honest.
Haiku
REHYDRATE THESE
GRAINS WAIT AND
HARVEST IN SILOS
FREEZER BAG MORALS
WHIR
I had a good run.

THWAK
Yeesss
m-a-a-g
m-a-a-g
Did I just hear you say...?

Remain calm, I heard a saying once "This too shall pass,
Trust me, Don't ask!
Where am I?
A TRAINEE HELPING YOU? I'm done!
Think... Potential.
Don't give up,

DO THEY HAVE TO START OVER?
But...
My formula could be improved
WHAT DO YOU SUGGEST?
~TH
Really learn from errors I always say
What then!
Meditation is a necessary tool n my job.
Yes
Always busy?

How did get in here?
We're the worst Prep team ever!
Thats so considerate compassionate thoughtful
I let the in! I was showing initiative, I thought.
Fat Chance
Can I...
leave?
I WANT TO SAVE THEM!
~maag~ ~maag~ ~MAAG~
Suggestion?

I've been working hard too!
Enjoying the planetscapes Aa
You didn't want me, it takes time... you'll see.
You'll appreciate me one day. Just watch Hh
Back to the petrie dish
Creations are unpredictable. Cutting our losses.
They aren't all bad
Am I supposed to witness this?
Nice
Do ever mature?
It's politics!

I GET THIS WAY WHEN... FRUSTRATED
~THWAK~
OH
No!
MEDITATING
~LURR~
~WHIRR~
VERY HUNGRY
DARN
Crop circles are a waste on YOUs.
I told them!

Look who slipped through
Oh!
Interesting business model. YOUs on display
Hi there!
Lets pretend intentional
NEVERMIND NOW!
WAS I SUPPOSED TO LOCK THE PORTAL?
TEAM FROM Gl'cpt!
This should be good
I HAVE TRANSFERABLE SKILLS!

Oh Joy!
This is my first mission
I brought [diamond symbol] with me because
Better lock that portal ...
Oops
Welcome!
Hi there! Hope I'm not interrupting
So much company!
I sensed to arrive early
We were just settling in.
Yes, you are early Buyer

Oh yeah
How did you get in Trainee?
Didn't lock the portal
I hope this isn't a problem?
I'm already nervous!
~ maag ~
I AM iSp
Yeah, lets mess with th
I AM Aa Team Leader!
~THWAK~
Two out of three members isn't bad.
Remember when we were compassionate?

Nothing personal!
Just what we don't need!
Hi! I'm new
Are you Kidding?
What do you mean by that?
Assets
... follow instructions!
I am a valuable asset!
HAIKU
STIRRING IS MOTION
SWIRLING VITAMIN
MAGIC. REPAIR POTTERY
Here we go again!
I follow sense

I can help, Really.
Like all I need is isp distractions!
That's okay
Done
DAIKU
AGAR AS BATTER
ALLURING STRANGE TASTINESS
ADDICTIVE SNACKING
Again?
And the cause of this testing is...
We are being tested

We are The prep Team. Valuable, Reliable, An example to others
energetic and committed to our roles and team members
We remain calm, focused.
Oh right, you're team leader
Don't say it.
Thank you Aa. As team leader I appreciate
Through bogus channels
Never let us forget
Glad you could join us iSp
Focus Team!
Close what? With what formula?

THAT'S THE JOY OF WORKING TOGETHER
We're so dissimilar
YES!
I WILL CHANGE THE SCENERY!
I'M HERE
Oops!
FORMULA?
Did I...?
I'M MELTING FAST
Lots of work to do! Stop melting!

YOUs
Note to Read Daanga like read manga. If un-familiar, do your homework!
BUYER
TRAINEE
~Maag~

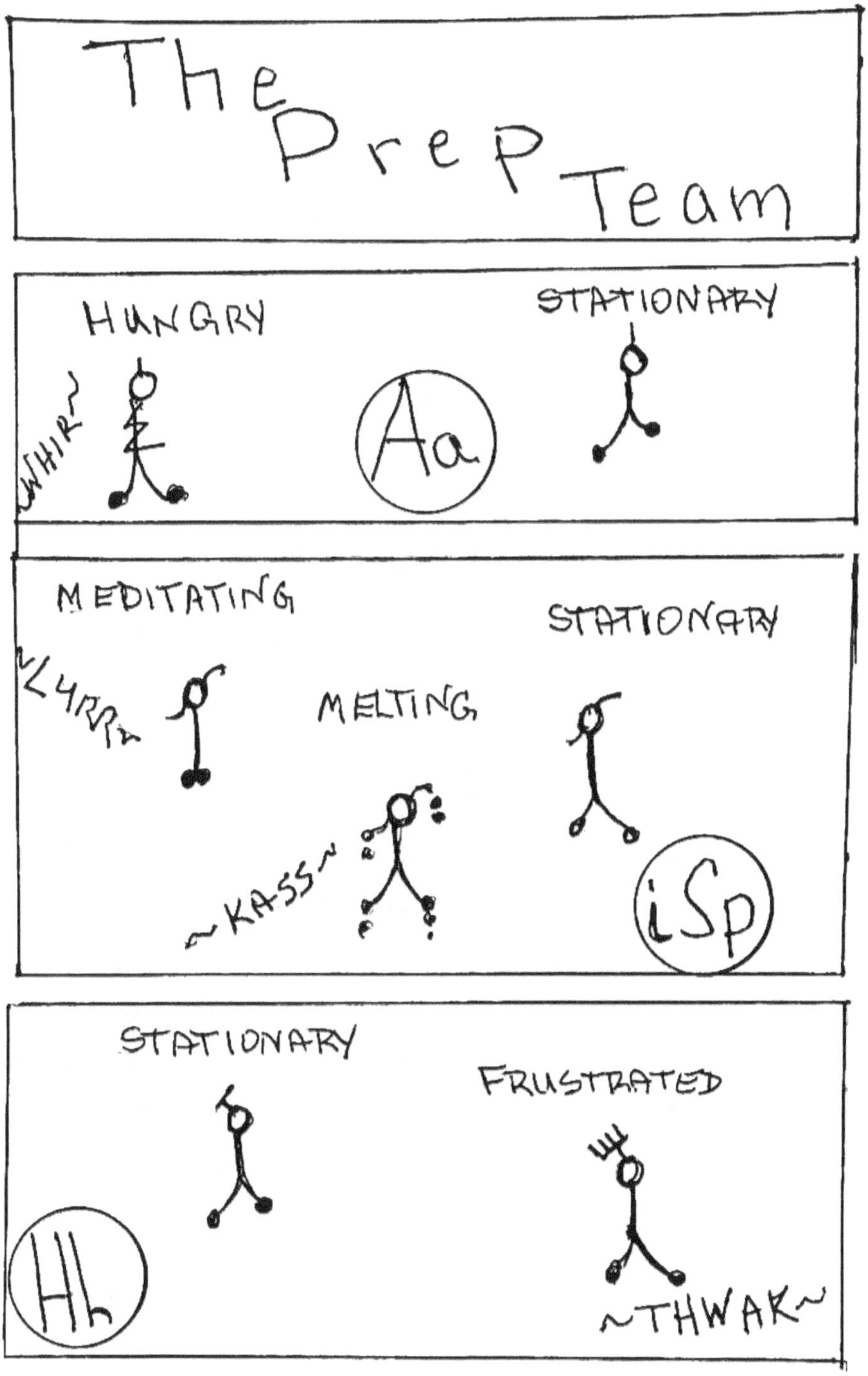
The Prep Team
HUNGRY
~WHIR~
Aa
STATIONARY
MEDITATING
~LYRR~
STATIONARY
MELTING
~KASS~
iSp
STATIONARY
FRUSTRATED
Hh
~THWAK~

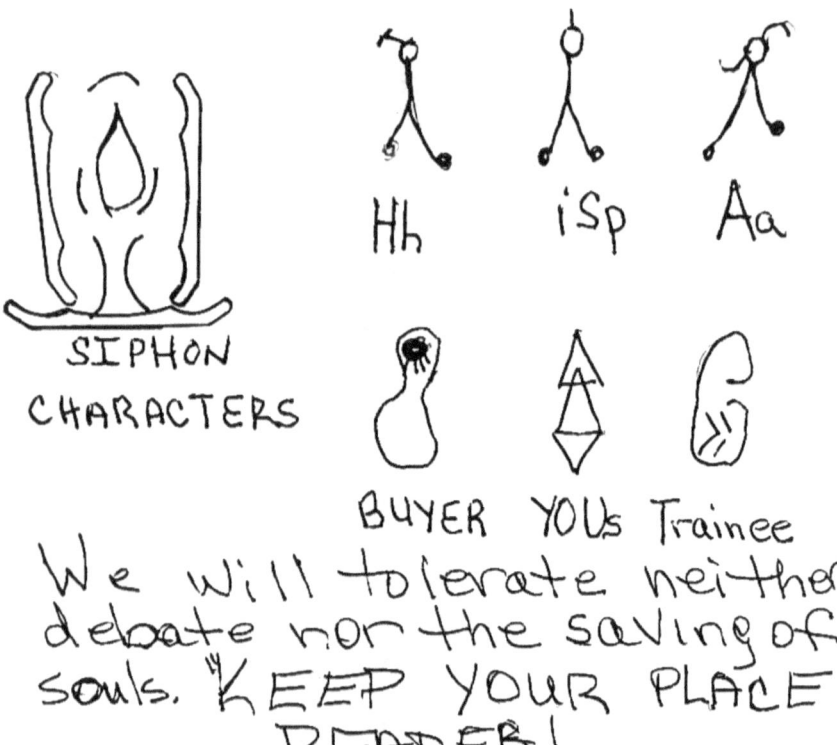

SIPHON
CHARACTERS

Hh iSp Aa

BUYER YOUs Trainee

We will tolerate neither debate nor the saving of souls. KEEP YOUR PLACE READER!

Data collection has been continuous, uninterupted work. Scenarios are experimental future settings. Daikus provide clues to the outcome Hh supervises, iSp is required by law due to difference and ability to develop scenarios. Aa creates release from tensions. Named others-Self explanatory.

SIPHON

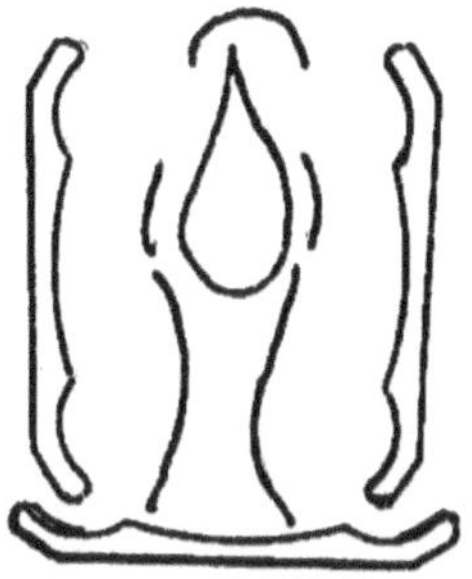

Text and artwork by Diane Murray Ward

DAANGA MANGA CHAPTER ONE

What are expectations? Some of us were told that this experiment was doomed from the start, others perservered. Here is the outcome, or is it?

Six characters will try to glean "the best" of this experiment. Introductions follow traits, sounds and roles. This is a mission for data retrieval only.

DANGA DIRECTIONS

"SIPHON" IS A DANGA*

DANGA IS READ AS MANGA.

TRADITIONAL JAPANESE MANGA

PAGES ARE READ

RIGHT-TO-LEFT

COMMENCING AT THE TOP RIGHT

OF EACH PAGE,

THEREFORE,

AFTER THE INTRODUCTION PAGES

READ DANGA ACCORDINGLY.

DEFINITIONS OF THE FOLLOWING FOR TBB: DAIKU, ECT.ETC., AND DIS.

Ect.Etc.:(Both accepted abbreviations of "etcetera" defining continuance) Ekphrastic work on sensory (touch, smell, sight, sound,) combined with nature, life, music, dance, movement etc. strung together with submissions building upon each other through time into infinity.

Daiku (Diane +Haiku): A haiku syllabic form but not discussing Gaia, but the nature of humans/food/situations.

DiS (Diane +Semicolon): An extension of the idea/story/message/quote YOU thought you finished, but not quite therefore, I'll complete that for you. You're welcome. DiS: "Younger LOVES Barley Bread Now" which I could have also named "Religious Jazz" aka "Do You Say Grace Before and After Meals? Aka "Do You Eat Ethnic Foods?"

ABOUT THE AUTHOR

Diane Murray Ward is a New Yorker of West Indian heritage.

She shares poetic/prose during national and international open mics, anthologies and is featured in podcasts.

She's a book reviewer, former modern-jazz dancer, blog-talk radio host and teacher.

Diane is an avid audience supporter for other creatives.

Her personal life, education and work experiences underscore her continuing engagement with creatives in several genres.

Diane is the recent co-author of a children's book published 2023.

Photo by ShiShotMe, Dorothy Shi Photography
Hat by Worth & Worth, Orlando Palacios
Jewelry by Beverly 'Sapphire' Wilson

A sample of Diane's works can also be found ...

"Nesting Straw" *Unsettled,* Benicia Literary Arts, 2024.

"Shivers" *American Graveyard, Calls to End Gun Violence,* Read or Green Books, 2023.

"What's Your Baby's Name, Bright Love?" *Tesoro,* First Anniversary, Firesingers, 2023.

"The Pieta Twice Beheld Her" *Another World Is Not Only Possible, But She Is On Her Way, International Women's Day Anthology,* Volume 2, ,stone Press, 2022.

"Can I Watch" *Fixed and Free Quarterly,* Vol. 1 Issue 3, Sept. 2022.

"Wounded Dreams" *Fixed and Free Quarterly,* Vol. 1 Issue 2, June 2022.

"Certainly Lord You See Side by Side Our Outstretched Hands" *Fixed and Free Quarterly,* Vol. 1, Issue 4, Dec. 2022.

"My Friends Call Me Salix B. Inc." *Love Letters to Gaia,* Miro and the Nuyorican Café Poets, 2021.

"Bring Your Own Candle" *Bronx Memoir Project,* Vol. 5, 2021.

"Grounded" *It's the End of the World As We Know It,* Red Penguin Books, 2021.

"Bouquet" *Bronx Memoir Project,* Vol. 4, 2020.

Nonogram Answer Key

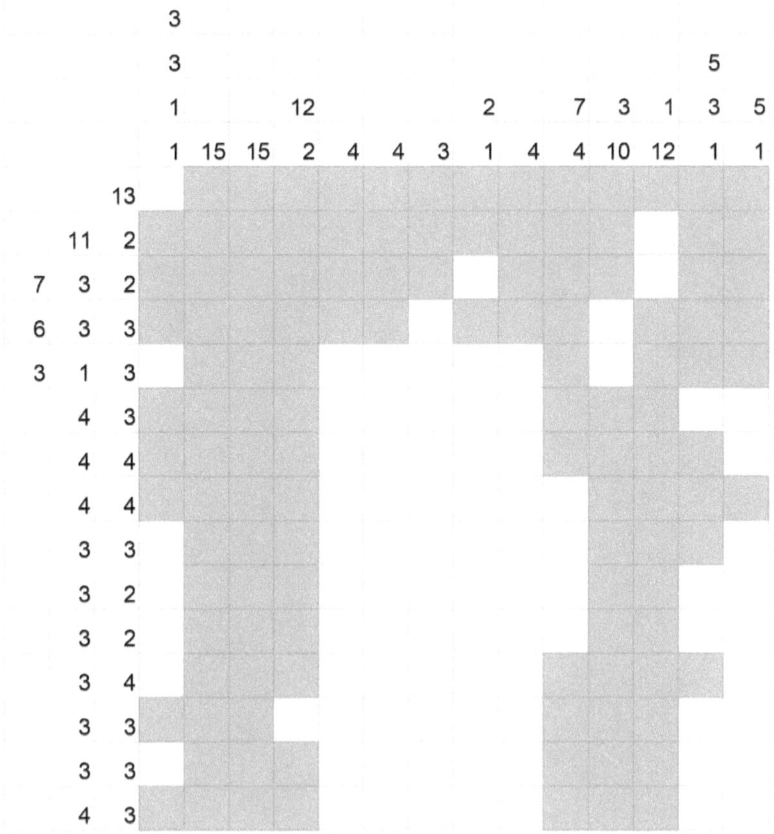

www.ingramcontent.com/pod-product-compliance
Lightning Source LLC
Chambersburg PA
CBHW030548080526
44585CB00012B/305